STUCK

Feeling Trapped. Breaking Free.

MARTIN A. BOWMAN

ISBN 979-8-88685-457-2 (paperback)
ISBN 979-8-88685-458-9 (digital)

Christian Faith Publishing
832 Park Avenue
Meadville, PA 16335
www.christianfaithpublishing.com

Printed in the United States of America

Contents

Preface

"*Help me! I'm stuck,*" *I said to absolutely no one.*

Feeling stuck! For those of us shackled within the clutches of this sensation, it is tangible and real! It is the *feeling* of being fixed tightly in a circumstance, a compulsive situation, or a position, unable to move despite repeated efforts. Unfortunately, because this feeling manifests in our thoughts, we often mimic the culture by misunderstanding its causes and symptoms, ultimately devaluing its validity. Yet feeling stuck has perceptible, identifiable reasons, clear biological markers, with corresponding neurohormonal activities in our brains. These biological activities trigger mental urges, behavior, and actions ranging from inappropriate, unwanted, devastating, and deadly. Humans are hardwired to undergo the biological responses that lead to feeling stuck. Consequently, since we cannot eliminate these urges, we must educate our awareness and consciousness to manage them, making them productive rather than destructive. Though drug/alcohol addiction is only the most egregious example of being stuck, fixations on overeating, using social media, playing video games, etc. are all indicators of addictive and compulsive behavior patterns.

> Trapped in my own body, uncomfortable in
> my own skin, sometimes I want to run away and
> see who will miss me! (Erica Slater)

Indeed, many reading this book are *not* addicted to overeating or drugs and alcohol. You're not frantically searching for a donut or a drug pusher / liquor store, yet all of us endure compulsive urges. Everyone is vulnerable to stress and trauma, and we all are susceptible to temptation. Unconscious routines will blindly usher us into habits we later discover hard to break even in everyday life. Every day we follow patterns, doing the same things without thinking about them. These actions aren't intentional, conscious choices but mechanical routines propelling our bodies forward in a kind of learned behavior. These are things done by habit, and when we try to break these habits, sooner or later, to some degree, we all feel trapped.

I

FEELING TRAPPED

1

I Feel Stuck

O wretched man that I am! Who will deliver
me from this body of death?
—Romans 7:24

Fear keeps you stuck. Faith sets you free.
—Shannon L. Adler

Frankie, a forty-three-year-old college grad and ex-championship wrestler from Torrington, Connecticut, lived in a local sober-living recovery house I supervised. In my fifteen years as a counselor/chaplain, he was my most enthusiastic client and a good friend. Working as project manager for a busy contractor in nearby Hartford, Connecticut, Frankie would talk nonstop, glowing about his twelve-year-old daughter, complaining about how infrequently his ex-wife allowed visits. Although I partnered with him through his recovery from alcohol addiction, Frankie was a leader, mentoring others as an active participant in Bible studies and twelve-step meetings. During these meetings, he spoke up frequently, studiously engaging our recovery curriculum, confronting his feelings of being caught in a compulsive cycle of substance abuse. He feared moving forward through sobriety and recovery only to return to a craving dependence once again. He said he often felt stuck.

In January 2021, after a raging argument with Frankie's ex-wife over money and visits, she again denied him cherished time with his daughter. Driving back home, Frankie pulled over, stopping for food and something to help him cope with his anger and emotional frustration. The following day, Frankie, my star pupil in the recovery curriculum, was found dead in his bed, having overdosed on fentanyl-laced drugs the evening before. Frankie had yet to adequately guard against the emotional triggers that would push him back to his old habits. Coping with grief, our community of recovering addicts was stunned and deeply disheartened by the fatal failure of one who once had such promise! There was this creeping sense that, just maybe, the journey toward recovery was doomed to catastrophe.

Stuck—that feeling of being caught in a mental trap, unable to move, incapable of change—is one of the most common, unspoken, yet depressing human emotions. We cry out for release—from our addictions, from the bondage of a cyclical habit, a destructive compulsion, only to find ourselves returning once again to the very thing that imprisoned us! The apostle Peter brutally refers to this condition as *"a dog returning to his vomit!" (2 Peter 2:22, referring to Proverbs 26:11). We feel stuck.*

Trapped

Feeling trapped begins as a nagging sensation, an aching feeling that we need to do something to change. We intend to break this undesirable habitual routine, propelling ourselves out of destructive habits—but we can't. We're frozen in a repetitive motion triggered by unknown, unrealized forces beyond our control. Substance addicts are a small portion of those struggling with feeling stuck. The broader state of cyclical compulsion is far more pervasive. In biblical times, stories about drunkards were overwhelmed by reports of hubris, lust, and sexual impropriety among men of every race and class. From Jacob and his twelve sons to King David, influential, accomplished biblical leaders at their peak crashed into corrupt dysfunction due to their inability to control cyclical arrogance and sexual passions. Managing our compulsions is the primary yet overlooked necessity for our long-term achievement as men and women. Frankly, we often fail because we do not focus on our need to manage our temptations.

But for most men and women, it's not the hubris of controlling dictatorial power that drives us to risky actions and bad choices. Most of us are just grappling with life situations, responding to isolation and boredom, struggling with feelings of inadequacy or shame, dealing with grief, mitigating our trauma, and medicating our pain. Often we dissociate from our memories whenever we experience shame, rejection, disappointment, assault, or physical/mental attack (i.e., traumatic stress) through coping mechanisms. We cope with our emotions and issues by seeking a distracting, comforting, or exciting experience in the form of substances, self-pleasing actions, and exploitive relationships. In short order, these actions become normative, addictive, and responsive to stress. Soon, without conscious thought or intention, we slip into a routine of habitual self-destructive actions now sealed and stuck in our psyche.

Again, being stuck is a feeling. Our thoughts create these compulsive cycles, sensations, and conditions. Our worldview, the lens cap through which we see our world, is established by those thoughts. These thoughts develop a pattern or paradigm, creating a running mental narrative supporting the thing that brings us comfort and justifies our rage. So, although everyone struggles, we begin to frame our work through the slippery slope of habit. Our habits create an aura of perceived safety within its boundaries only to discover that security limitations are a prison trapping you. So once we are caught in the cycle, its power is magnified. Subsequently, our brain pushes the thought that we have no hope.

What's worse—we live in such a social-media-controlled, advancement-focused, me-oriented society. Frankie was an extremely effective construction executive, a top earner at his firm, well-liked, and had a stellar future. He had strong self-expectations. We highly value achieving our dreams and overcoming the barriers that block us. It's no surprise we lapse into acute depression when we sense no progress in moving forward and, in fact, revert to the same old habit that held us back. This feeling of being trapped, caught in repeating cycles of addiction, unable to change or escape from something, makes us feel, well, *stuck*! Undoubtedly, actual changes to neurohormones in our brains pre-accompany these feelings and cravings, yet we can alter this neurological component through therapy, rehabilitation, and medical assistance. But even when physical desires leave, mentally there remains much work still to be done. The battle is *always* in our minds. I work specifically with recovering substance abusers attempting to endure the mental challenges and responses to life conditions that can yank them back into substance usage.

I know a bit about feeling stuck in cyclical, repeating habits. Years ago, while working as a young construction project manager, I developed a severe drug habit that seemingly could not be broken. Countless rehabs and numerous twelve-step programs I attended were a never-ending routine of desperate attempts to release from this bondage, but upon sober self-examination, it soon became apparent that drug abuse was just one of the myriads of bad habits I struggled with. Profoundly immature, I lost countless jobs, promotion opportunities, and eventually, my first wife and kids. Yet through it all, I always believed I could stop—until I couldn't. Though resolute in my determination to quit my habit and rebuild my life, I always seemed to revert, like that dog returning to his vomit. Back in my old neighborhood of Brooklyn, New York, we used to say, *"I was stuck on stupid."*

The psychological disciples discussed in this book will work for any compulsive urge beyond drugs and alcohol just as well. With rates of relapse among recovered addicts so high, these recovery techniques save lives. I pray that you will read and discuss these techniques with others on this journey. If you are likewise struggling with compulsive cycles, let this book be a vision of hope arising. The more you understand about the trap, the more you will be able to break completely free. This story is about the process and journey to break those regular cycles and achieve transformative release.

2

The Roots of Our Compulsive Spirit

Please, Lord, make me pure…but just not yet!
—St. Augustine

There are known knowns and known unknowns. But there are some things we know we do not know. And then, there are also unknown unknowns, the ones we don't know we don't know.
—Donald Rumsfeld, former US Secretary of Defense

For Meagan, it was a familiar routine—she noticed her dresses didn't fit as they used to because of added weight. As a middle-aged single Christian woman, her appearance was a constant source of concern. Her back problems made the extra pounds more burdensome. In response, she had gone through the litany of fad diets and lifestyle-change programs. Meagan would often get on social media, proclaiming that the old had passed, the "new" had come, and this time, she would transform into a new svelte self—only to yo-yo back to her original figure. Distressed and regretful, she felt stuck, caught in cycles of despair, unable to change. Why can't she simply stick to her diet? How did she end up stuck in a compulsive cycle? How does she change and get unstuck?

Even though humanity is in perpetual pursuit of new revelation, there are many things about which we remain ignorant and unaware. As Donald Rumsfeld stated above, we don't know what we don't know. Sadly, we can only change what we are aware of. In her book *Good Habits, Bad Habits*,[1] social psychologist Wendy Wood claims we can spend 43 percent of each day doing things without ever thinking about them. She writes:

> Almost half of our actions are not conscious choices, but the result of our non-conscious mind nudging our body to act along with learned behaviors—
>
> - how we respond to the people around us;
> - the way we conduct ourselves in a meeting;
> - what we buy;
> - when and how we exercise, eat, and drink.

Without realizing it, every day we do many things automatically, unconsciously, outside of our awareness, simply by habit. When we consciously determine to change these tendencies, we rely upon our willpower then struggling in our conscious being, mustering up the determination and intention needed to effect positive results. The devout Christians among us resort to fervent prayer and healing messages in hopes of miraculous transformation, yet confronting repeated failures, we experience many emotional reactions such as frustration, depression, anger, and self-deprecation. These are the roots of that feeling of being stuck.

The Roots

> *Now the works of the flesh are evident: sexual immorality,*
> *impurity, sensuality, idolatry, sorcery, enmity, strife,*
> *jealousy, fits of anger, rivalries, dissensions, divisions,*
> *envy, drunkenness, orgies, and things like these.*
> —Galatians 5:19–21(NIV)

---

[1] Wendy Wood, *Good Habits, Bad Habits: The Science of Making Positive Changes That Stick* (Farrar, Straus & Giroux, 2019).

The tendency toward our compulsive spirit, the roots of our bad habits and addictions, began literally at the beginning in the garden of Eden. Living within the garden's splendor, Adam dwelled in harmony with the Spirit, enjoying its fruits—love, joy, peace, patience, kindness, goodness, faithfulness, gentleness, and *self-control* (Galatians 5:22–23). Note that the last fruit of the Spirit, foundational in its placement, is self-control. Our emotions and feelings—required to enjoy fruits such as love, joy, peace, etc.—are tempered and regulated by our ability to self-control. Theologically, when Adam and Eve "fall" to temptation, they lose control over their easy self-restraint. Suddenly lust, fears, envy, and selfish passions overtake them, releasing their vulnerability to the "works of the flesh."

In biblical terms, the flesh is emotion without the prompting of the Spirit. Because of our feelings and passions, the "flesh" thinking seems logical and correct. Further, what we sense as purity and integrity seem dull and boring, dampening our youthful pursuit of fun. Paul interprets this dilemma as our need for a Spirit to help us "capture" our emotions and thoughts to bring them into obedience to Christ to flow in the fruits of the Spirit. NYC Pastor Dr. A. R. Bernard describes our need to "educate" our emotions so they can bless us as intended. We struggle, he surmises, with uneducated emotions, suggesting that our task is, quite simply, to begin a process of taking our emotions to school. My mother would often complain that I lacked self-control despite my Ivy League and graduate school education. Dr. Bernard would more accurately label my problem as immaturity. But following the spirit, the sign of my maturity was not a function of age and experience but a part of understanding the behavioral factors that held me back and those that would propel me forward.

Vipers in diapers

As infants, the development of our emotions primes us for its miseducation. We were born with a predisposition toward emotion-dominated thinking. For example, a relative newborn infant experiences joy long before it has a fundamental understanding of it. The infant hears and senses comforting sounds and sensations that result in positive responses. In fact, over time, the baby experiences sadness, fear, anxiety, satisfaction, and peace, and long before it understands those emotions. Its brain doesn't yet comprehend any logical progression of rational thought or reason. The baby simply reacts to what is seen and felt. Thus, the emotional parts of our brain form long before the thinking part of our brains. Put simply, we could "feel" long before we can "think." Consequently, our emotions easily override our rational thought processes, subverting reason, logic, and morals. From the time we are infants, gravitating to single-minded, selfish desires, we can be demanding "vipers in diapers."[2]

Our mind naturally gravitates toward what brings selfish pleasure; we incorrectly connect our satisfaction and happiness to what brings pleasure. But, by contrast, happiness should be the achievement of a state of peace, and peace is defined as not simply the absence of conflict; it is the absence of conflict with the *presence* of order and justice. Shalom, the ultimate blessing in the Judaic tradition, was not for happiness but for peace upon the household. Thus, only when you are at peace are you pleased in any lasting sense. I don't mean to trash the concept of pleasure, but by definition, *pleasure*, in our immoral world, is a narcotic, a dangerous opiate for compulsions that can quickly rebound into addictive cycles. We relate pleasure to our emotional state. Thus, each event we experience, each incident we endure, and each new piece of information we intake has surrounding emotions attached. Without a mature process of digesting information, emotions fall within a spectrum from depressive trauma at one end to uncontrolled pleasure at the other extreme. Without educating our feelings, left unchecked, these emotions begin to direct our thinking, guide our feelings, determine our direction, and thus, control our lives.

---

[2] Voddie Baucham, *Wretched: The World, The Flesh & The Devil* (Ligonier Ministries, June 9, 2019).

Unconscious habits

> *Excellence is not an act but a habit.*
>
> —Aristotle

Maturity is vital in this change process because habits are not universally bad. Aristotle rightly declared that excellence is a habit, not an action. However, the constant blare of advertising directed at women, displaying waiflike, perfect bodies, the self-perpetuating pressure from social media, and the persistent preaching by well-intended pastors and motivational speakers magnify our failures. We're told to have faith, believe in ourselves, and be encouraged. Then when we publicly fail, we sink into private shame.

Why can't we change our inappropriate, compulsive behaviors? Is it because we aren't trying? Why can't we summon the willpower to "just do it?" Surveys have shown that among certain groups, 81 percent claim lack of self-control was their reason for relapsing back to old bad habits. A 2011 survey called "Stress in America"[3] showed that 27 percent of respondents believed lack of willpower was the most significant barrier to change and the primary obstacle to losing weight or staying off drugs. Although we believe in miraculous change as Christians, the church is often notorious for creating faith expectations that skew the psychology of achieving sobriety and weight-loss goals. Frankie was avid in his Christian faith, outwardly confident, active in his twelve-step meetings, and outspoken in pursuing his sobriety. Meagan displayed passionate determination and desire. She had relied on prayer and peer support. These were the spiritual guardrails she believed would be enough, yet secretly, she suspects her willpower is insufficient and her faith is weak. Mentally beaten, she became resigned to her condition.

The problem is that our cogent observations are not always entirely rational. Under stress, we quickly underestimate, remaining unaware of factors that control our behavior. We all have influ-

---

[3] Norman Anderson, CEO, "Stress in America. Our Health at Risk" *American Psychological Association* (released January 11, 2012).

ences, biases, preferences, triggers, and traumas that cannot easily be undone. Further, we tend to overestimate our rational ability, failing to understand, actually ignoring our irrational selves. Although Jesus came to save us, his most important work was his efforts to reset our patterns of thought. Quite simply, he came to change our thinking! This book will examine psychological disciplines and techniques in our journey to break those habitual behavior cycles and achieve transformative release.

"But I have *changed!"*

Many reading this text will push back on the theme of this book, arguing that decisiveness and willpower can work in changing behavior. There have been times when you were scared and insecure. You have overcome your fears, making a decision, spurred by focus and motivation, yet these past achievements of behavioral change are often "one-off" situations. Often tangible short-term success in affecting temporary behavior change misleads us into underestimating the goal of *achieving long-term change*. This book is about *maintaining* change. We stress the persistence, the repetition of actions amid competing forces, which is the key to more extended success. When our desire for something is strong, we can muster the focus and endure doubts and naysayers. We start that diet, quit that drug, and change from nagging, inappropriate behavior. Our fear and insecurity will push and motivate us into action, resulting in momentary success and claims of victory. We feel proud and convinced that our willpower works for all things.

The point of this book is that breaking free from feeling stuck involves syncing our goals to our habits. Unfortunately for many, we've fallen into the old drug dealers' trap of thinking that we have this under control. Pushers gladly give away their product's first "hit" and dose, knowing that this path leads to our addictive cycle. Our nonconscious mind has tricked us into believing it is easy to break a bad habit. Research has shown that our minds can accomplish these "one-off" actions and temporary changes to our behavior. Sustaining the behavioral change, particularly those habits borne from trauma, is far more complex. The start of a good practice does not, in any way, indicate the sustained, repeated effort required to turn an action into a routine, achieving lasting change. Your nonconscious mind has tricked you into believing that it is easy to break a bad habit.

The challenge of change and growth

> *Growth is painful. Change is painful. But nothing is as painful as staying stuck somewhere you do not belong.*
> —Mandy Hale

Struggling with her weight gains, Meagan recalled the mental pain of staying stuck in an "undesired space." The desire to change means much more than leaving the known past—the plump body, the addiction, and the bad habits. Positive change is equivalent to growing into an unknown state. We remember the advertising mantras (i.e., "just say no" to drug use or "just do it" to exercise) as rude reminders of our frustration of living in the spaces we despise. The inevitable change happens to us, out of our control. It is growth that seems elusive, almost impossible to achieve. We are passionate about our desire to lose weight, but that donut appears to call us through the vista of time. We perceive unconsciously slipping into states of urging, subject to forces pulling us into destructive cycles. The cycles and routines are predictable and straightforward. It is a pattern based on comfort for the moment even if that moment, over time, turns into misery. We eat the donut because at the moment, it is comfort food. It satisfies our mental and physical urgings. Just seeing the donut triggers memories of its taste, generating desire. We are protective of the simple things that reinforce our "stuckness." We are tied to an unconscious routine we do not even realize. You cannot change behavior cycles that you are unaware of.

> Change is inevitable, but personal growth is a choice. (Bob Proctor)

Meagan was able to effect more sustainable, long-lasting changes to eating habits when she intentionally linked these changes to a lifestyle of healthy living, which included healthy eating. Meagan refocused her thoughts on losing weight, denying her urges to snack to pursue a healthier lifestyle. She joined a vegan cooking class, planned her meals weekly, linked her morning prayer groups with exercise and stretching routines, and searched for tasty yet healthy food products to fulfill her snacking urges. She spent far less time putting pressure on herself on social media, mentally bolstering her consciousness for the long haul of healthy living. She consulted a counselor and began to observe her routines, identifying the emotional triggers she confronted when undergoing job stress and dealing with family. She began to develop a procedure for breathing, calming herself, and trying to reduce stress when these situations occur. Meagan laughed, admitting she tended to cope with stress by indulging in sweet potato pie and other delights. Although pressure on the job pushed her to high productivity, it pulled her off any healthy eating discipline. Her priority shifted from dieting to stress management and calming disciplines when she endured unavoidable stress.

Meagan explained that the "pain" of maintaining a problematic discipline is far less than the mental pain of stagnant living. Often, stepping forward into transformation and growth means stepping back from our perception of safety. It means challenging our unspoken, unrealized routines we rely upon to cope in comfortable and safe ways. The comfort foods we eat make us feel secure. Even for the addicted, getting high means getting to a place of perceived safety. Intellectually, we know that getting high is not safe, but tangible feelings of security come from the familiar routine, the comforting actions, and the cyclical patterns of activity that will ultimately kill us. These feelings of security are the definition of comfort zones.

Finally, this challenge of behavioral change and growth for the addict can be challenged by the prevalent "disease" concept of drug recovery. The misunderstood platitude repeated by addicts and counselors is that addiction is a disease. Indeed, addiction does have components of a disease in that there are biological markers that run adjacent to neurological activities associated with addiction. However, embracing this concept allows the addict to embrace the excuse that addiction is an illness without self-responsibility. The danger is that when an addict believes they are not responsible for addiction, the recovery process devalues self-responsibility in behavioral change. A mature understanding of substance abuse acknowledges that I am responsible for my abuse actions, which empowers me to the revelation that I am, likewise, accountable and able in my recovery. Change and growth are painful but possible. Faith (i.e., belief in things I cannot see) is essential to produce the evidence of things hoped for. Thus, the apostle Paul complains, praising his thorn in the flesh:

> Or because of these surpassingly great revelations. Therefore, to keep me from becoming conceited, I was given a thorn in my flesh, a messenger of Satan, to torment me. Three times, I pleaded with the Lord to take it away from me. But he said to me, "My grace is sufficient for you, for my power is made perfect in weakness." Therefore, I will boast more gladly about my weaknesses so that Christ's power may rest on me. That is why I delight in weaknesses, insults, hardships, persecutions, and difficulties, for Christ's sake. For when I am weak, then I am strong. (2 Corinthians 12:7–10)

Leaving the comfort zone

After a thirty-two-year career as a systems engineer and sales executive at IBM, Virginia Marie (Ginni) Rometty was stunned when offered to ascend to the chief executive's office. A woman had never been CEO of a Fortune 500 company, particularly one renowned for its blue-suit, white-shirt conservatism. Mulling this offer, she confided in her husband that she felt "not ready," ill-prepared to assume such a demanding position. Challenging her, he asked would she feel the same if she were a man. He pointed out that boys are raised to take risks, to accept challenges while girls are expected to be sober, patient, and reserved. For Rometty to run with the "big boys," she would have to change her inbred mindset, embracing risks and challenges.

> I learned always to take on things I'd never
> done before. Growth and comfort do not coexist.
> (Ginni Rometty, CEO of IBM)

Rometty had excelled as general manager of IBM Global Services Division, expanding and absorbing major consulting firms while growing their "cloud" and cognitive computing businesses. Yet despite all her accomplishments, she couldn't see herself in a position dominated by male executives. She later remarked that most people remain stuck because our formula for achievement and success is distorted by a natural penchant for familiarity and comfort. She would famously state, *"Growth and comfort do not coexist."* When change does come quickly, we tend to underestimate and take it for granted, leading to long-term reckless, destructive actions. Indeed, growth certainly deserves celebration, but staying in your comfort zone often means you are not growing. Rometty discovered that her main challenge living outside of her comfort zone was the danger of being cut off from support systems and mentorship. She stresses taking small steps, building on previous experiences while not protecting the past. She urges that we play to our strengths, always looking forward while reflecting on past mistakes. Since we cannot control the inevitability of change, we can control our reactions to change. Our supreme focus is our growth from change regardless of whether that change is good or bad.

3

Trapped in the Dysfunctional Community

They promise them freedom, while they themselves are slaves of depravity—for people are slaves to whatever has mastered them.
—2 Peter 2:19

The Healing at the Pool

Now there is in Jerusalem by the Sheep Gate a pool called in Hebrew Bethesda, having five porches. In these lay a great multitude of sick people, blind, lame, paralyzed, waiting for the moving of the water. For an angel went down at a particular time into the pool and stirred up the water; then whoever stepped in first, after the stirring of the water, was made well of whatever disease he had. Now, a certain man was there who had an infirmity thirty-eight years. When Jesus saw him lying there and knew that he already had been in that condition a long time, He said to him, *"Do you want to be made well?"* The sick man answered Him, "Sir, I have no man to put me into the pool when the water is stirred up; but

while I am coming, another steps down before
me." Jesus said to him, "Rise, take up your bed
and walk." *And immediately*, the man was made
well, took up his bed, and walked. And that day
was the Sabbath. The Jews, therefore, said to him
who was cured, "It is the Sabbath; it is not lawful
for you to carry your bed." He answered them,
"He who made me well said to me, 'Take up your
bed and walk.'" (John 5:2–11 NKJV)

I grew up thinking this story was just another healing by Jesus.
In fact, a famous Negro spiritual, *Wade in the Water*, was taken
directly from these verses. Unfortunately, this story is another indica-
tion of my immaturity as a Christian. Like many, I had an image of
Jesus as meek and mild, miraculously healing the poor and afflicted.
Yet despite the 150 healing stories/scriptures in the Bible, this is not
one of them! A mature reading of the story shows a stern Jesus confronting, even jarring, the psyche of an invalid and observing wit-
nesses, pushing them into constructive action. Jesus himself never
actually does the healing. Instead, this story portrays a man stuck
in a compulsive personal struggle, surrounded by a community of
people stuck in similar efforts, all feeding into the same self-defeating narrative. It's about fighting temptations and the disease of bad
habits that have us bound to addictive routines. It's about an entire
community trapped in a chronically traumatic environment for so
long that they've started grasping at useless popular myths, a sort
of prosperity gospel. They've been mastered by the crushing depression of their condition, unable to take the most straightforward steps
to walk toward authentic healing! They've all tried to get healed by
their willpower but, sadly, have failed; and now, they are trapped
in a dysfunctional environment—a community of "the stuck"! It is
tragically common for a community and environment to take on
the depressing characteristics of its residents. Thus, there is a cyclical
reinforcement of the feelings of depression and trauma each resident
experiences.

For context, the pools at Bethesda were two-tiered public baths located by an entry gate in Jerusalem's great wall. This entry gate would be used by Jewish pilgrims carrying their lambs for ritual offerings at the feast of Passover. Thus, this continual parade of lambs through this gate generated the label "Sheep" gate. *(It seems prophetic that the Lamb of God always entered through the Sheep gate!)* Traditionally, communal bathing pools were a final opportunity to clean up before encountering temple priests with lamb offerings. So great was the tired, dusty crowd at Bethesda that the second pool of equal size was built adjacent to the first. The two rectangular pools, built side by side, formed a large structure with columnar porches around the perimeter and a porch running between the two, creating five porches. Often tepid dirty water of the pools would be replenished by clean water from an onrushing flow of underground pipes of an aquifer relief spring, yet a local legend claimed this dirty water recycling was an angel stirring healing water into the pool. Thus, an anxious throng of ragged invalids gathered at the pool perimeter, forming a ghetto of impotence. Impotence implies that everything one needs is present, but it will not work. This community was described as blind, lame, and paralyzed, or those who can't see, can't walk, and thus, feel immobile. Feeling stuck, they've been drawn here by the fantasy of the "healing angel" legend. *Bethesda* in Hebrew is translated as a house *(beth)* of mercy or grace *(saida)*. So paralyzed with immobility, these folk frantically waited for the healing lottery year after year!

The frustration of years of futility has pushed this desperate community to a classical "prosperity gospel." Notice in the legend that only a single person gets healed when the angel arrives. Like crabs in a barrel, feeling powerless, everyone else was left to scheme, push, and shove in a truly chaotic scene. This self-destructive scene was the antithesis of a cooperative, beloved community sought by the ministry of Jesus.

> For an angel went down at a particular time
> into the pool and stirred up the water; then who-
> ever stepped in first, after the stirring of the water,

was made well of whatever disease he had. Now, a certain man was there who had an infirmity thirty-eight years. When Jesus saw him lying there and knew that he already had been *in that condition a long time, He said to him, "Do you want to be made well?"* (John 5:4–6 NKJV)

This question *"Do you want to be made well?"* sounds silly or condescending at first. Why does an all-knowing Jesus ask such a ridiculous question, knowing that the condition has lasted thirty-eight years? People are at the healing pool to be healed, right? Realize when God asks a question, it's not because He doesn't already know the answer. *He asks these questions because he wants to make us think.* He confronts us, pushing us to look inward and reconsider our actions (repent) and self-defeating thought processes. God demands sightless faith as well as engagement of our reasoning and thought process. Instead, we become coconspirators of our bondage. Through self-examination, we realize that *even if we are victims*, our reaction to external forces has caused internal paralysis, a self-directed "stinking thinking."

When confronted to look inward, we often blame others, deflecting and ignoring our part in the paralysis. This moral self-judgment defies our instinct to seek affirmation/approval, know and be known, and be liked. We're terrified of revealing our deepest secrets and shortcomings and, thus, present a veiled image, masking our true selves. Disguising our hurts, addictions and compulsions, embarrassing faults and weaknesses and our vulnerabilities, our "stuff" remains buried behind a mask, festering and multiplying like an unchecked fungus.

Worse still, the local church often does not help, acting hypocritically. "Church folk" can destroy people inside and outside the church while secretly struggling with similar issues. Often, like homosexuals in the military, we "don't ask, don't tell." The church sets a standard of holiness that is admirable and scriptural, yet when we compare ourselves to the bar, we fall short. Realizing our ugly nakedness, we are ashamed and hide *(remember Adam's reply to God)*.

We move forward like nothing ever happened, knowing deep within our consciousness that we are less than what we outwardly appear. Thus, sitting in church, we live in caves of secrecy, with all of us having something in us that we don't want to be exposed. But there is healing in hiding. Author John Ortberg once wrote, "*You cannot be fully loved unless you are fully known.*"

The community surrounding the pool at Bethesda had come to embody its immobility and negative characteristics. Designed initially as refreshing, a bathing pool, Bethesda transformed into a dreadful place filled with dysfunctional, paralyzed people. So suffocating was this environment its residents spent time moping around, waiting to "hit the number"—a lottery ticket out of impotence when an angel came. The pandemonium would consume these ragged, desperate folk clamoring to be the first in the water! It is into this chaotic scene that walks a disapproving, irritated Jesus!

> The sick man answered Him, "Sir, I have no man to put me into the pool when the water is stirred up; but while I am coming, another steps down before me." Jesus said to him, "Rise, take up your bed and walk." *And immediately*, the man was made well, took up his bed, and walked. And that day was the Sabbath. The Jews, therefore, said to him who was cured, "It is the Sabbath; it is not lawful for you to carry your bed." (John 5:6b–10 NKJV)

Jesus shows clear disdain and displeasure watching the chaotic scramble of invalids. The typically humble, demure Jesus practically screams at the invalid man. "*Rise!*" he shouts, eventually demanding that he leave none of his stuff behind. Then he sternly commands, "*You! Walk!*" Jesus offers no comforting, tactile embrace, no caring hug, no anointing with oil, no spit into the mud and rubbing his crippled legs. He provided none of the liturgical gestures and tricks of the process we often see in our church healing services. Where is the Jesus we've come to expect in our immature discipleship? But

Jesus wisely realizes the nature of this condition is such that if it miraculously disappears, in due time, it will cyclically return. We want to bury our issues still alive. *When you bury your conditions and personal issues alive, burying it without honestly killing it, in due time, it will resurrect again* at the worst possible moment to wreak havoc in your life and the lives of your loved ones. Sometimes buried stuff renews in a differing manifestation of the original but with the exact root causes. Sadly, with our masks in place, we are convinced we have conquered our demons. Thus, Jesus, the healer, cannot heal our wounds.

Confronted with a demand to self-examine, the paralyzed man ignores the question, blaming everyone around him. He refuses to look at his own culpability, implying, "*I* would *get well, but* they *won't help me.*" Just like Adam in the garden of Eden blaming the woman God gave him, our condition is always someone else's fault. A frustrated Jesus tries to get us to take ownership of our circumstances, freeing us to be a source of recovery rather than a cause of dysfunction. Everything this man needs to recover, change, be made well, and emerge from bondage is already within.

Finally, motivated by this stern command, the invalid rises on his own, walking forward, returning only to pick up his mat. He has doggedly changed behaviors and habits in a dramatic spectacle, with everyone witnessing a "miraculous" recovery, yet the journey only begins with attaining change. Now he must *maintain* the shift! We stop our destructive habits when the consequences of our actions become unbearable. Directly delivered, we praise the Deliverer, embracing the spectacle of dramatic conversion. It makes an excellent church service! Yet the audience is full of naysayers and eye-rolling family members who've seen this movie before. At Bethesda, everyone witnessed this man's condition for thirty-eight years, knowing only his one identity—a paralyzed invalid. The church elders (Jewish temple officials) knew him well, resulting in their condescending demeanor. So imagine this man, now healed, confronting the icons of his faith, who inform him his healing was illegitimate! Your behavior change cannot be totally dependent on supportive families or the community. That is probably why Jesus had this man return to get his mat—so it would not remain a trigger option for relapse.

The community may be the problem, *but the community is also the solution.* It is vital that a person changing a habit or condition intentionally seek a *supportive* community, reinforcing the journey of change. Though you can't change your family or the neighborhood you reside, you can seek a network of wise counsel, sponsors, and mentors to whom you can be transparent and accountable. I tell my fellow recovered addicts that you cannot stay sober in isolation although you must stay away from people who benefit from your addiction. Whenever you feel the urge, when you want to run to a bottle or a drug, run to a sponsor or a mentor.

Unfortunately, our battle against bad habits, destructive tendencies, and traumatic self-defeating actions often has become normative. In effect, we are used to the problem, not the solution. The invalid lived in that condition for thirty-eight years. Often our conditions have become our self-identity. The invalid had no name or identity other than "the invalid man" or the "paralytic." Like the "addict," he's been in this condition for so long that his condition, his description, has become his name! Many people grow up in households full of invalidity, psychological paralysis, alcoholism, abuse, low expectations, hearing derogatory words, etc. Our "habit," our compulsion, is how we deal and cope with lives of trauma. Achieving freedom from these destructive cycles moves from the comfortable dysfunctional known to a terrifying unknown.

4

—————

Fighting Temptations: Why Billy Can't Help Himself

No temptation has overtaken you that is not common to man.
—1 Corinthians 10:13

Lead us not into temptation.
—Matthew 6:13

Our initial decisions, the free-will choices to consume a drug or alcohol, initiate a behavior, and take action, are not addictive or compulsive. Our decision to *return* to this consumption, behavior, or step in a repeating cycle can quickly become obsessive and addictive. The greatest threat to achieving real victory is not failing, fear, or even doubt but controlling our compulsion to satisfy ourselves. Self-gratification is the most powerful tool that the enemy uses to entice and tempt us into short-term pleasure and long-term misery and destruction, keeping us from fulfilling our destiny. That addictive/compulsive behavior is man's most crippling bondage, not the prisons. So why can't we change? Why do we feel so stuck?

Back in the garden of Eden, Eve and Adam took a bite of the fruit from the tree of *knowledge* of good and evil. Suddenly, that *knowledge* made them vulnerable to and recipients of potent, natural compulsions toward "sin" of self-satisfaction. Suddenly, their focus was on themselves, the creation, and not the Creator. Suddenly, they began feeding those compulsions, doing what makes them feel good, avoiding what was uncomfortable or painful. They began to act naturally, not spiritually or obediently. Soon they were in bondage to their compulsions, and those natural inclinations zoomed out of control. Soon *"they just couldn't help themselves."*

Before Adam sinned, he had that last fruit of the Spirit, *self-control.* Once he fell, he lost his self-control and became subjected to the passions, the lusts, the pride and ego, the "soul-rashness," the heat of the flesh. He naturally sought to regain his control over his environment without the knowledge and direction of God *but through his knowledge.* Man, now in a state of natural uncontrol, seeks to bring his background under control. He seeks power; he seeks the satisfaction of self. Humanity naturally seeks to control its external setting, and when he cannot do it with the fruit of the Spirit, he will do it with the works of the flesh.

Aside from robust mental responses and compulsion when exposed to certain environmental situations, actual biological or natural events occur within the body that complicates this struggle. Medically, hormones and adrenaline-like substances in the brain are secreted, or released, at external stimuli such as when you see, hear, touch, smell, or taste certain things. You can just think about certain things and images, memories, etc., and these substances release, causing the sensation of solid compulsion toward certain behaviors. Further, 20 percent of Americans suffer from abnormalities in the brain's management of serotonin and norepinephrine, bringing overwhelming feelings of gloom and doom, leading to America's most widespread disease—depression. Often, we attempt to correct these feelings with substances and inappropriate behaviors. Finally, men receive a chemical pleasure high from erotic mental images that release a hormone called epinephrine into the bloodstream. This substance locks into the memory the illusions of happiness from past events. Even if the past event wasn't that great, the memory accompanying this hormonal release is always fantastic. We become addicted to the feeling and unconsciously crave the release of this hormone.

Essentially, the John 5 "Healing at the Pool" story is about our failures at fighting temptation and vulnerability to compulsive habits. Those who read this may not all be alcoholics and addicts, but absolutely all of us are vulnerable to compulsive habits, and we are terrible at fighting temptation. Compulsion is a chronic and long-lasting disorder in which a person has recurring thoughts and resultant actions that a person wants to change but cannot. The Bible says that Jesus *"was in all points tempted as we are, but without sin" (Hebrews 4:15).* Although Jesus, in his humanity, was a master at fighting temptation, we rarely study his teaching for strategies for dealing with our compulsiveness, yet we all struggle with something. Realize that if Jesus was tempted, no amount of anointing would insulate *you* from temptation. So we must learn from the man.

We are tempted by the very habits we've determined to change. These repeating cycles of negative, sinful habits and lifestyles contribute to our inability to change. All those bad habits—smoking, taking drugs and alcohol, overmedication, overeating, masturbation—all those little things that for us spell relief! These sins are not the dramatic, horrific acts but the little puppy foxes that grow over time into ferocious wolves. These characteristics often cause us to act out in seemingly harmless, irresponsible ways resulting in compulsive cycles challenging to change. We are emotional beings who live, as the Bible says, in our "flesh." Apostle Paul states clearly in Romans 7:

> The power of sin within me keeps sabotaging my best intentions; I need help! I realize that I don't have what it takes. I can do it, but I can't do it. I decide to do good, but I don't do it; I choose not to do wrong, but then I do it anyway. My decisions, such as they are, don't result in actions. Something has gone wrong deep within me and gets the better of me every time. (Romans 7:17–20, The Message)

Every human will struggle with temptation and compulsiveness, which will not change. As Paul is stating, we can often come to the point of mental frustration. Instead, the Bible commands that we learn to manage our compulsiveness by developing spiritual disciplines. This, in effect, establishes positive compulsions in place of harmful compulsions. Realize that we all struggle with some area of our flesh, but the struggle is not the sin. The actual sin, the tragedy, becomes accommodating to the evil, developing a comfort with the evil, thereby getting stuck in the cycle.

A theologian once explained that he considered "sin" a one-time act. By contrast, "iniquity" is a repeating, continuous sinful act (i.e., the cyclical act). As a young man, the devil wants to attach an iniquity to you so that you can carry it into maturity. When no one cares, that bad habit you have will grow and prosper with you as you grow and prosper. Consequently, what we struggle with at forty-five years old actually began in our teens and twenties. So, what is the thing you said you would never do again—only to return like the dog to its vomit? What is the thing you know God wants you to let go of? Often it's something sexual or some addiction—like uncontrolled anger or unreasonable impatience. Many of us love God but suddenly realize we are caught in something, some repeating, cyclical habit or act. If we didn't love and believe in God, it would not matter, yet we know God is not pleased with us deep in our hearts. If everybody sins and fails, then how do we get back up? You get up and move forward when you stop making excuses, blaming others, and examining and understanding how you started this cycle.

It is normal to pray for strength and help for your unbelief. *But maturity demands that we stop praying to God to do the things God has told us to do for ourselves.* Indeed, God does something to a certain point but expects us to take over; or when we step out in faith, confronting the unknown, unsure of how or why we will succeed, God will reward our loyalty with miracles and unforeseen circumstances that make our way clear. When we feel stuck, we have to stop sitting by the side of the pool, waiting for some angel or miracle to make the problem go away.

"My sin, my sin! Please don't take my sin!"

The human personality is like a charioteer with two headstrong horses, each wanting to go in different directions.

—Plato

The word *sin* has become such an impersonal King James-type word that it has little meaning today. We have difficulty admitting that our compulsive behavior hurts anyone, destroys our future, or blocks our future achievements. In fact, for many of us, our "sin" is our best friend. I am not referring to sins like flying jet planes into the World Trade Center. This sin easily entangles us (Hebrews 12:1) as the things we crave and take ownership of. This is "my sin, and I wouldn't do it if it didn't make me feel good." "My sin" is how I spell relief, the thing I turn for escape and fantasy, filling the empty places inside me. As long as we persist in denying that this sin controls our lives, we will not stop. Failing to see the long-term destructive consequences, we will only see its immediate gratification, its short-term burst of pleasure. Therefore, simply trying to "not do" that sin is agonizing. When we try to stop, we try to "not do" the exact thing we want to do, and that is agony. It is hard to kill what we love.

> For the good that I will to do, I do not do; but the evil I will not to do, that I practice.
> (Romans 7:19)

You have to find something positive and productive, something enlightening, something encompassing to do that will sustain you and motivate you, not simply relieve you and make you feel better. You have to come to invest in some short-term pain to gain what exalts you long term. You will be faced with choices that feel good now and seem too hard to achieve and too good to believe. Faith comes into the strategy, and fear/doubt enters as its chief competitor; and when you deal with those choices, you have to give up what you cannot keep, gaining what you cannot lose.

Nibblin' sweet grass (the lust of the flesh)

*You don't need to go out this morning saying that Martin Luther King
is a saint. Oh, no! I am a sinner like all God's children. But I want
to be a good man. And I want to hear the voice saying to me one day,
"I bless you because you tried. It is well that it was in thine heart."*
—Martin Luther King

On March 3, 1968, a month before his assassination, M. L.
King Jr. returned to his father's pulpit at Ebenezer Baptist Church
after a time of personal reflections on his sexual infidelities. The man
who spoke the words "I have a dream" would now deliver a poignant
counterpoint to that sentiment in a sermon entitled "Unfulfilled
Dreams."[4] With disturbing self-pity, he would admit, *"God knows his
children are weak and weary."* He referred to the pull of lust, using
the analogy of a lamb aimlessly caught up *"nibblin' sweet grass"* as the
wolf lurks in the shadows, ready to attack and devour this unaware
little beast. His analogy implies we are innocent and blameless when
trapped in lust actions, yet we realize we aren't entirely blameless
deep in our hearts. Please recognize that the purpose of this book is
not to condemn but to awaken and alert us to the power of forces
that seek to control us while giving strategies to overcome them.

> There is a civil war going on, a schizophre-
> nia, like Dr. Jekyll and Mr. Hyde. There is this
> tension, within all of us, between good and evil.
> (Martin Luther King)

Lust has been called the beast lurking and prowling within
the loins of humankind, but more importantly, it has captured and
ravaged the deep inner recesses of our minds. Lust covers a broader
menu than sex including power, fame, attention, etc. Lust is the most
powerful of the compulsive desires, remaining deadly poised such

---

4   Martin Luther King Jr., "Unfulfilled Dreams," sermon at Ebenezer Batiste
    Church (Atlanta, Georgia: March 3, 1968).

that when we suppress it in our actions, it continues to rage in our thoughts. It emerges, ugly and burning, from its hiding place, thinking we are safe, smirking at our arrogance. We want what we want when we want it. Though we may be too "proper" and "sanctified" to manifest into that beast outwardly, it is there within the souls of all humanity; and until we confront that beast and understand how to control it, it will counteract our attempts to tame it.

Preaching to family and friends at the church where he grew up, King tried to describe a civil war inside his head. He pointed to the tension between good and evil raging in his heart, transparently connecting to Paul's words, *"I see and approve the better things of life, but the evil things I do."* As a generational icon chosen by God and history to affect change, King agonized at his inability to stop returning to his lustful compulsions. Though he could motivate the hearts and minds of generations, he felt stuck in a trap; and now his friend and biographer, Vincent Harding, recalled King confessing how deeply he had failed himself and his own best possibilities.

At its core, lust is satisfying the self at the expense of God and others. It is the preoccupation with what the self wants. This is the satisfaction, the gratification of the flesh—compulsive desire based on wanting, seeking to take and self-satisfy. We connect our concept of love to our obsessive desires, often saying we love the thing we desire, yet we are describing our lust more than love. True love (i.e., God's love) is always giving. Despite what we may believe, God's love desires to satisfy the object of his love. When God's purpose for our lives begins to manifest because of the struggle and confrontation internally and externally, we think he must not love us. This is the paradox we confront. If he loves us, we secretly want God to make life easy for us.

Yet a loving God sets us on a path requiring confrontation of our doubt, fear, and sometimes mental or physical pain. Reading about God's beloved son agonizing in the garden of Gethsemane verifies this conundrum: *"For God so loved the world that He gave His only begotten Son."*[5] Love is all giving, no take. Lust wants to take. It

---

[5] John 3:16

wants to "get" and is selfish. We better get honest about our passions, selfish desires, and sexuality and stop crying smugly that "we have it under control." We need to fill our minds with God's Word and pray a prayer casting down imaginations, any high thing that exalts itself against the knowledge of God. Don't be afraid to "choose the narrow path."[6] Be *accountable* to Christian friends for your actions. Remaining unaccountable in our efforts can lead us to step blindly into a deep river.

---

[6] Matthew 7:13–14

5

Relapse Prevention: Examination and Techniques

There is enough stuff in me to make both gentleman and a rogue.
—Johan Wolfgang von Goethe

The tragedy of relapse

I awoke one hot August morning in 2011 to a headline—*"Prominent Black Pastor dead in swank NY hotel."*[7] Zachery Tims, the forty-two-year-old televangelist, the founder of the 7,500-member New Destiny Church in Apopka, Florida, was found dead in his room at the W Hotel with a packet of white powder in his pocket. This was a tragically familiar story during my many years as a drug counselor. Tims, who had heroically escaped crime, violence, and drug addiction in the eighties as a Baltimore teen, had tragically returned to clandestine drug usage by the early 2000s. Following a familiar pattern, he fell into infidelity, losing his marriage to his copastor wife in 2009. Eventually, the NYC chief medical examiner declared what my colleagues and I suspected—Tims died of "acute intoxication by the combined effects of cocaine and heroin." This was yet another spectacular relapse—a disastrous return to old destructive behavior after

---

[7] *NY Daily News* (August 12, 2011).

a successful recovery, critically depressing to many still struggling in drug recovery.

Relapse prevention

"Relapse" is a behavioral phenomenon commonly used in substance abuse vernacular, yet clinically, it is defined as the recurrence of *any* disease (cancer, for example) that had gone into remission or recovery. Thus, most chronic diseases (heart disease, cancer, diabetes, and addiction) are subject to periods of relapse. For substance abusers, the cyclical return, the "craving" feeling/urges that are normal in the abuse stage, will reoccur after treatment and a process of withdrawal/cessation of this behavior. Most who struggle with cyclical adverse behavioral patterns, once exposed to certain trigger occurrences and risk factors during their recovery, risk returning to the negative behavior. As Christian rehab programs and church support groups are now touted as more effective than secular, the task of relapse prevention counseling has become a growing part of the pastor's/chaplain's purview. Zachery Tims's fall from grace notwithstanding, more and more churches and Christian missions offer recovery support groups/programs and AA meetings, with programs such as Celebrate Recovery (offered in thirty-five thousand churches in the US) dominating the curricula used.

Yet relapses to unwanted human behavior in all areas stubbornly persist among congregants and the evangelized. What care and preventive approaches should the pastor offer that assists members and converts in coping and overcoming this growing problem? After achieving it through the long discipleship process, how do we maintain good behavior?

Problem

Relapse and risk are a significant part of treatment and recovery from life-controlling issues. A 2014 study in *JAMA*[8] reports that

---

[8] *Journal of the American Medical Associations* (2014).

between 40 and 60 percent of people treated for substance addiction and alcoholism will relapse within one year of treatment.[9] Further, while relapse is most common in the first year of recovery, persons with years of sobriety often resume self-destructive behaviors, drug use, or drinking. Thus, some prototype of Twelve-Step Facilitation (TSF), traditionally called AA, or Alcoholics Anonymous, is now applied to over three hundred addictions and psychological disorders such as smoking, sex and pornography addictions, social anxiety, overeating, compulsive spending, problem gambling, etc. Over one million persons now attend some sixty thousand meetings worldwide, yet despite AA's claims to the contrary, results seem to be poor.

In their book of twelve-step programs,[10] authors Dr. Lance Dodes and Zachary Dodes write that

> Peer reviewed studies peg the success rate of AA somewhere between five and 10 percent (of those who complete the program.) Actually, less than 1 in 15 people who enter these programs is able to become and stay sober.

Factually, many enter the programs, never staying beyond a few meetings. The *Alcoholism Treatment Quarterly* reported in 2000 that 81 percent of newcomers stopped attending meetings within the first month while by ninety days, the figure rises to 90 percent. Bottom line, a 2007 internal survey of AA members showed that only about 30 percent of active members stay sober for more than a decade.[11] Thus, with a huge failure rate, relapse back to destructive behaviors remains a major issue for counselors—Christian or otherwise. Without understanding the reasons for relapse, it is impossible

---

[9] Ruben Castenada, "Why Alcoholics and Addicts Relapse So Much, It's the Brain Chemistry" *US News and World Report* (4/24/17).

[10] L. Dodes. & Z. Dodes, "The Sober Truth: Debunking the Bad Science Behind 12-Step Programs and the Rehab Industry" *Boston Press* (2014).

[11] **Jake** Flanagin, **"The Surprising Failures of 12 Steps: How a Pseudoscientific, Religious Organization Birthed the Most Trusted Method of Addiction Treatment,"** *The Atlantic Monthly* (Mar. 24, 2014).

to develop strategies for preventing this cyclical behavior. First, let's examine the popular treatment options intended to prevent relapse.

Faith-based vs. secular relapses prevention

Celebrate Recovery, a faith-based recovery program birthed from California's Saddleback Church in 1991, directs its ministry to a wide array of dependencies and compulsive behavior including the alcoholism suffered by its founders. It claims a success rate of nearly 85 percent although I am suspicious of the validity of this rate. Yet faith-based recovery/treatment methodology remains statistically more effective in practice than the secular programs due to logical reasoning. Firstly, *all* twelve-step methods rely strongly on a group dynamic of encouragement and accountability to others that reinforces the methods used and keeps the individual from talking themselves back into resumption of destructive behavior. However, faith-based groups emerge from settings of positive group dynamics, stressing a strong external guiding force. Secular groups, like many AA/NA groups, rely more on testimony and storytelling dynamics of other addicted subjects. Secular groups rely on repeated admission of the past—"*I am an addict.*" By contrast, faith-based groups do start with admission of past truths but quickly shift, anchoring on a future vision (i.e., a faith-based vision casting of victorious overcoming). This horizon vision of life without the controlling influence powers personal interactions, instructions, and exhortations between clients and facilitators in the faith-based groups. Thus, "Celebrate Recovery" predicts success while Alcoholics Anonymous reminds of the affliction.

Alcoholics Anonymous

Alcoholics Anonymous[12] and offshoots are the dominant international small-group fellowships with two million members worldwide belonging to over ten thousand groups. It is designed as a fel-

---

[12] www.aa.org

lowship of alcoholics/addicts helping others similarly afflicted with achieving sobriety and maintaining recovery using the twelve-step facility. Interestingly, the founder, William Griffith Wilson, known as Bill W, claimed to have cured his alcoholism through divine intervention and not scientific methodology, yet at meetings, newcomers are asked to become "friends of Bill," referring to his AA name of Bill W. This was intended to provide the easy rapport and environment needed to become transparent among those you may not know well, others also in need of help.

Historically, Bill had a traumatic upbringing, struggling with depression and panic attacks causing serious problems at his salesman work and among social groups over many years! Alcohol abuse emerged as Bill's means of coping with the pain and trauma of his mental struggles, a common theme in many compulsive drinkers. Finally, in 1934, an old drinking buddy, Ebby Thatcher, shared with Bill his success at maintaining sobriety through the guidance of an evangelical Christian outfit called Oxford Group. Curious but unconvinced, Wilson continued drinking until hospitalized with potentially fatal acute alcoholism. At Charles Towns Hospital for Drug and Alcohol Addictions in NYC, Wilson fell into an extreme fit of depression during a testimonial visit from Thatcher. Suddenly, Bill began crying to God for his own release from alcohol bondage, witnessing a "white light" transformation that resulted in joining Thatcher in never going back to drinking again!

Although Bill's dramatic spiritual experience was more typical of charismatic 1930s evangelical tent meetings, Wilson began to share his testimony. He joined Thatcher's Oxford Group and began using his salesman skills to help other alcoholics. However, Bill was initially unsuccessful at convincing others, almost relapsing himself during his battle with depression. Fortunately, another Oxford Group member, former alcoholic named Dr. Bob Smith, intervened to encourage Wilson to remain sober. The influence of Dr. Smith allowed Wilson to mentally connect his spiritual experience of awareness of his compulsive condition with the practical tools of medical and physiological methodology for *maintaining* sobriety. Apparently, Smith had several relapse episodes and became interested in establishing a methodology for maintaining sobriety and warding off relapse. By 1938, Wilson and Smith's work with small-group therapy among alcoholics led to the publication of a book entitled *Alcoholics Anonymous*, listing the twelve steps for spiritual growth[13] into sober and spiritual health. Thus, this small movement of therapeutic small groups took on the name Alcoholics Anonymous, adopting the twelve steps as required guidelines across groups.

By the 1950s, the movement had grown as the popular alternative treatment methodology. By the 1970s, Congress passed the "Comprehensive Alcohol Abuse and Alcoholism Prevention Treatment and Rehabilitation Act,"[14] adding legitimacy to this methodology as a primary treatment process. By the turn of the twentieth century, as state and federal budgets were allocating multimillions of dollars to treatment of substance abuse and chemical dependency, the twelve-step methodologies are the preferred treatment despite its flaws and misleading, overhyped success rates. Judges typically refer previously incarcerated to twelve-step programs as an alternative to sentencing or as a condition of probation. Yet once again, most relapse occurs over the course of a year beyond treatment.

As has been demonstrated, most addiction and destructive compulsive behavior causing cyclical substance abuse and relapse is closely linked to emotional dysfunction usually derived from trauma episodes. Second, all persons, particularly addicts, crave positive supportive community, yet addicts and alcoholics universally share that the wider culture persists at stigmatizing, shaming, and devaluing addicts, addiction, and the compulsive behavior. This is the self-delusion that denies that everyone struggles with compulsive behavior. Social stigma pushes addicts and alcoholics into small groups like AA even if the methods offer extremely poor success rates.

---

[13] W. Wilson, R. Smith, *Alcoholics Anonymous* Fourth Edition (AA Grapevine Inc.).

[14] Extensive public hearings on alcoholism were held in 1970 by the Senate Committee on Labor and Public Welfare, which then reported S. 3835, Comprehensive Alcohol Abuse and Alcoholism Prevention, Treatment, and Rehabilitation Act.

Celebrate Recovery

Founded in 1991 by John Baker, an elder at Saddleback Church, Celebrate Recovery (CR)[15] has over twenty-seven thousand persons who have completed its course, with five million completed at the thirty-five thousand satellite sites. The small groups are led by strict curriculum and trained CR facilitators vs. the untrained group leaders of AA. Although there can be incidents of proselytizing, this faith-based approach broadens its client focus to underlying emotional health and trauma issues ("hurts, habits, and hangups") that, if remained unaddressed, would allow relapse. These faith-based groups understand that stress, anxiety, depression are prime causal factors leading to codependency and compulsive behavior. Thus, a compulsive disorder that manifests as addiction to drugs can easily transfer to other destructive behaviors such as overeating, "oversexing," etc. The more one is aware of the roots of their compulsion, the better they are able to manage it. Beyond the Bible study and prayer, there is journaling, meditation, and individual/group therapy sessions with Christian counselors. Instead of the "Big Book" of AA principles, there is a Life Recovery Bible that includes the twelve-step model. These standards include a workbook that allows clients to write and process their thoughts with regard to traumas and process feelings under the guidance of the chaplain or facilitator.

After a thorough review of these program documents, both secular and faith-based, avoiding relapse can be summed by three main areas: (1) awareness and avoidance of trigger events; (2) establish positive networks of friends, encouragers, and mentors; (3) remain in consistent therapy and/or discipleship. Thus, relapse prevention (RP) must become a "cognitive behavioral approach" involving identifying and managing the high-risk situations that trigger obsessive-compulsive behavior. We crave community but relapse is most often caused by exposure to people, places, things and emotional reactions that drive/distract recovered abusers off their plan. The distractions are

---

[15] www.celebraterecovery.org

usually stress, anxiety, anger, and lust that causes arousal, rage, moodiness, and isolation.

It is impossible to avoid the trigger events that arise from everyday interactions with family and work/social interactions. The faith-based facilitator is there to assist the client in managing these events. By example, the riskiest event for the former substance abuser is the passing of a loved one. Mourning this loss is a massive trigger event that certainly cannot be avoided and must be managed so as to avoid spinning back into relapse. The chaplain mentors the clients through these events, providing perspective and clarity to endure the pain of loss without relapse. Together, the chaplain and client process anger or traumatic memories triggered by current events.

Relapse prevention plan

The relapse prevention plan is the primary tool for allowing a client to plan his/her immediate actions when a triggering event happens. It causes a focus on personal behavior and establishes action items one can undertake to refocus from a distracting event.

The stages of relapse

In every relapse, there is a process despite the identity of an event that triggers. Relapse itself is not an event but a process that advances through stages. The method may begin weeks or months before the event of a literal relapse. The steps are emotional, mental, and physical.

a. *Emotional Relapse:* In the initial emotional phase, hormones present in the brain are secreted when stimulated by certain specific situations, determine/control (profoundly influence and persuade) what the brain is interested in doing. In the ideal world, neurohormones help guide social, sexual, mating, parenting, protective and aggressive behaviors. However, the world is not perfect! Our emotions and the behaviors they generate set us up for a possible relapse. A baby experiences joy, sadness, stress, and anxiety long before it understands these emotions. The baby's brain has not learned remotely what it is to think or reason with any logical progression, yet the baby can feel the whole range of emotions. Thus, the emotional part of the brain is formed before the thinking part of the brain. Humans learn to feel before learning to think, causing emotions to override thinking, reason, and logic. Thus, humans must learn to manage emotions (be taught) to understand (and control) these emotions. We associate an emotion with every piece of information we receive. We remember information surrounding an event relative to the emotion surrounding it. Many substance abusers tend to desensitize and become emotionless. The chaplain attempts to educate the emotions because they are actually meant to bless us, but left uneducated, emotions begin to direct thinking, guide feelings, determine the direction, and thus, control lives. Signs of emotional relapse include withdrawal, isolation, and depression. At this stage, the pull of relapse gets more robust, and the sequence of events moves faster.

b. *Mental relapse:* Mental relapse is the argument that rages in the mind. The thoughts are focused on using as the means for coping with the emotions the people, places, and things that accompany the usage of substances. There is a "glamorization" and fantasizing of the past use. As the pull of addiction gets more robust, it becomes easier to give in to the urge and plan accordingly simply.

c. *Physical relapse:* The journey from thought to action for a struggling addict in recovery is small unless drastic technique and intervention occur. Without intervention, all of the client's strength and drive are directed toward relapse, not prevention. Short of imprisonment, there is no achieving abstinence through brute force.

Substance use and stigmatization of mental health

The American Psychological Association reports[16] produces evidence that is already widely known—that African Americans, Hispanics, and Asians are least likely to treat or even acknowledge mental illness such as depression. In fact, beyond the cultural stigma, any socioeconomic group enduring poverty, homelessness, crime, joblessness, etc., are more likely to suffer mental illness or develop depressive psychological disorders due to long-term coping with these conditions.

The unwillingness to treat these usually undiagnosed mental conditions or even be aware of the effects of long-term trauma dramatically increases the probability of substance use as a means of coping. In certain areas, it is normative. Drugs and alcohol are a way of life throughout the world in specific communities. As substance usage has shifted from illicit (cocaine, heroin) to legal corporate-produced substances (opioids, alcohol), the demographics of use and addiction have skyrocketed. Unfortunately, the substances have skyrocketed in purity and deadliness. Today and every day this year, every eleven minutes, an American will die of a drug overdose,[17] killing almost one hundred thousand persons in 2020. In the state of West Virginia alone, Big Pharma has produced more lethal doses of opioid pills than there are people living in the state.

A young woman in my Newark mission was diagnosed with early-onset bipolar and borderline personality disorders in her early teens. After gentle prodding, I found that she had been sexually abused as well, yet she was academically gifted, graduating with honors from high school and college. Her struggle with social and emotional skills disrupted her work history and pushed her into homelessness. Sexual

---

[16] Mental Health: Culture, Race, and Ethnicity: A Supplement to Mental Health: A Report of the Surgeon General, Substance Abuse and Mental Health Services Admin. (Aug. 2001).

[17] www.thetruth.com

promiscuity and substance usage were when the mental health system failed her. Prescribing more pills provides a temporary Band-Aid without the therapy and counseling that an Alcoholics Anonymous twelve-step will not begin to feed. I found that simply allowing her to release and share her story built the trust between client and facilitator that accommodated her entry into a long-term woman's recovery program. Three years later, she has graduated and has been working ever since while in transitional recovery.

Although many recovery resources are available while persons struggle with overt addiction, the transition back to life in recovery is the most critical period for maintaining sobriety. Unfortunately, this young woman got into a romantic relationship that ended in disaster. The heartbreak of this breakup triggered a relapse event that resulted in an overdose. Without a counselor or group to partner with her, she fell back on the crutch that had helped her through past traumas. She died at thirty-four years old, another urban tragedy that led to the writing of this book.

Early relapse prevention

The first step is being aware that events have pushed the client into extreme risk no matter how long the client has been in recovery. As a client slips into emotional relapse, the client must avoid isolation. Clients can talk themselves into anything. The client must recognize the anxiety and practice relaxation techniques and self-care. Practice self-care. Resentments and fears, typical in all emotional relapses, must be relieved through some form of relaxation.[18]

Techniques for dealing with mental urges

Glamorizing and fantasizing presume that the client can control usage. Counselors preach, "Play the tape through." Every addict knows that one indulgence will lead to many more. Playing the tape to its logical conclusion causes the fantasy to become a nightmare.

---

[18] www.addictionsandrecovery.org

Calling a friend, support, or someone in recovery is a significant step toward prevention. Anything to distract from the emotional spiral is positive. Finally, the client must do their recovery one step, one moment, or one day at a time. If the client waits thirty minutes, usually the urges dissipate. Slow down the emotional spiral. Feelings of anxiety and stress are exhausting. No matter how difficult, relaxation allows a client to be more open to change.

As simple as it sounds, relapse prevention replaces destructive urges with good ones. Our bodies and minds were designed to respond to cyclical patterns whereby the repeat of action builds our tolerance and craving for that action. This process was intended for our growth and discipline in building our tolerance to positive development patterns. This is like an athlete working out or a bodybuilder repeating reps with weights. However, trauma and immaturity push humans into destructive cycles. Consequently, the chaplain/facilitator is like a coach working out his athletes in positive processes of physical as well as mental development. We are training and educating our client's emotions and behaviors.

II

BREAKING FREE

6

Perseverance

*I have fought the good fight. I have finished
the race. I have kept the faith.*

—2 Timothy 4:7

Finish the race

The 1968 Olympic Games was a colorful, widely televised inter-national spectacle with iconic star athletes competing in the oxy-gen-depleted air of mile-high Mexico City. American gold medal winners like Bob Seagren, Bill Toomey, Al Oerter, Dick Fosbury, and Bob Beamon were household names. Political and social controversy arose as two-hundred-meter runners Tommie Smith and John Carlos stood on the medal podium with their fists raised in black-gloved defi-ance. Yet the game's most poignant, lasting figure was an unknown African runner competing in the brutal 26.2-mile marathon who finished dead last. Factually, fifty-six runners began the marathon while just under thirty-five struggled to finish at University Stadium. Mamo Wolde from Ethiopia crossed the line first, followed by Kenji Kimihara of Japan and the rest of the crowd.

After the marathon medal ceremony, as runners returned to their lodging and television crews packed up the equipment, a remarkable sight appeared at the stadium gate. A lonely disheveled runner appeared, jogging slowly in a torn, muddied uniform, bandages on his legs and blood on his arms. Struggling to complete the last few steps of the marathon, several amused observers looked on in disbelief, snickering at the sight of this stubborn runner. Collapsing at the finish line, someone put a microphone to his face, asking who he was and why he was still running long after the race was technically over. He replied, "*My name is John Stephen Akhwari from Tanzania, five thousand miles away. I did not come all that way to start a race. I came five thousand miles to finish a race!*" Finish the race indeed.

Over fifty-five years later, Akhwari's words, "*Finish the race,*" have become the heart cry of every person confronting a difficult task. Akhwari claimed to have never considered abandoning the race despite sheer exhaustion and bloody falls along the course. His dogged determination has been chronicled in countless documentaries about his will to finish. In her research on willpower, Dr. Angela Duckworth labels this human trait as "grit." As a middle school teacher in NYC, she had noticed that the ablest and most intelligent students weren't always the most successful. Accomplishments and learning were not simply the result of high IQ but were strongly dependent on motivational and psychological factors. The students who performed the best had a personality trait she called grit. Her 2016 book *GRIT: The Power of Passion and Perseverance*[19] defines *grit* as the ability to keep working toward a goal, overcoming challenges, and sticking with it even when it's hard. Thus, less talented people can achieve success, reaching long-term goals at higher rates, despite setbacks, hurdles, and failures. A work ethic of repetitive, relatively simple tasks done over time leads to sustaining growth more consistently than the dramatic events we tend to embrace. Tiger Woods points to his work ethic—long boring practice sessions as a youth day after day in rainy, stormy weather—as the prime key to his success.

Setting ambitious goals requires planning and awareness of a long process. Smaller makeable steps done repeatedly with little visible progress are the standard for achieving goals such as losing weight or quitting drugs. We can achieve success and change our

---

[19] Angela Duckworth, *GRIT: The Power of Passion and Perseverance* (Scribner, 2016).

behavior for a while, yet attaining short-term wins can disguise the difficulty of maintaining this success. We need to prioritize replacing bad habits with good habits. Like addictive bad habits, good practices are cyclical, repetitive behavioral actions that build over time to maintain the desired goals. We can dream of changing our behaviors, getting married, or starting a business. Maintaining the behavioral changes, the marriage, and business determine its success.

Failure factor

> *Winners fail until they succeed.*
> —Robert Kiyosaki

> *Success is the result of perfection, hard work, learning*
> *from failure, loyalty, and persistence.*
> —Retired US General Colin Powell

Every difficult achievement involves trial and effort, trying, and occasionally failing but trying again. Grit does not mean never failing or thinking of quitting. Failure is part of the process of success. If you are determined to succeed, be prepared to fail and learn from the experience. *Grit* is defined as continuing the routine despite failures and setbacks. When our steps are small, setbacks are likewise minor. If you encounter no setbacks or failures, your goals are not aggressive enough. Despite testimonies to the contrary, achievements don't depend on a miraculous cure. We can pray for miracles, but we must get busy doing the necessary work. Amid this work, moving forward to the impossible goal, miracles will pave the way.

> Defeat is a state of mind. No man can be defeated until defeat has been accepted as a reality. (Bruce Lee)

There is no failure except a failure to try. Legend says Thomas Edison endured ninety-nine failures before the hundredth attempt produced the lightbulb. Albert Einstein wrote that failure was simply success in progress. Sir Isaac Newton technically failed at discovering the theory of relativity until Einstein made corrections and reset the understanding of the theory, winning the Nobel Prize for physics. Instant success is a myth in the mind of the naïve observer. The process is long and brutal, repeating attempts that seem to fail along a path toward building to success. Perseverance is a character trait. The actual procedure for achieving the lasting goal is a period that will not be shortened. If we want to achieve the goal, we have to endure the time and expend the effort. We focus on the vision of the endpoint, the harvest, to water our seeds of faith. When we stop watering the seeds, they will always die. We must stop looking for spiritual resurrection for things we have long stopped feeding and watering. Defeat does not mean you are defeated. Giving up means you are defeated. Resilience through failures is developing the grit to succeed.

Distracted by talent

> *For though the righteous fall seven times, they rise again,*
> *but the wicked stumble when calamity strikes.*
> —Psalm 24:16

I idolized Willie Mays, Jim Brown, and my favorite, Julius Erving. Later, entrepreneurs like Henry Ford and Steve Jobs captured my imagination. Our American society is defined by hero worship, using terms like *genius, talent,* and *hero* to describe the iconic business, music, and sports stars. Videos of great "hero" moments run on social media in continual loops, generating millions of views. Talent has become our way of explaining a person's success. Talent means that we, less talented, cannot compare ourselves or think to compete. We are awed by the media visuals; we believe talent and exceptional ability are the only ways to accomplish complex tasks. Unfortunately, this trend devalues character as the necessary ingredient to every accomplishment—from quitting drugs and losing weight to scoring touchdowns and hitting home runs. When a motivation coach stresses character as the undeniable quality for achieving success, the smirks appear, and listeners' eyes begin to roll.

Character, as a personality trait, is universally misunderstood and debased; yet complex tasks cannot be achieved without resilience and perseverance, the primary character traits. Understand that talent and ability are inherited gifts. By contrast, character traits are built. Confronted with failure, people murmur, *"I don't have what it takes!"* But character is not something that you have or get. It's something that you *build*. Everyone can make these traits. Think of character as a muscle we must develop and develop. We work out as an athlete, building this muscle through repeated usage and work. Even Michael Jordan admits others have been born with more basketball talent. He will stress that he has worked and developed *into* his greatness. The significant accomplishments are "done" with hard work, not magic. Even "rocket science" is trial and effort. Three words to remember are

Greatness is doable! (Angela Duckworth)

Thomas Edson once said that genius is 1 percent inspiration and 99 percent perspiration. If athletes don't practice, training their muscles, no matter how gifted, their accomplishments will succumb to another who worked harder and more intelligently. The key to losing weight and quitting drugs is not the magic pill or talent and ability. The key is simply to work at developing grit. Work the process of setting goals, encountering challenges, enduring setbacks, powering through, and trying again—and again. Like the fable of the tortoise and the hare, a person with character will overwhelm the person with talent every time. However, this effort is not a competition. Whether losing weight or quitting drugs for good, we need the support and encouragement of a select few around us. Many may critique us while enduring the struggle, but find a few who will celebrate us.

Stuff happens

> *Your Daddy was a drunk. Your Momma was*
> *a drunk. You will always be a drunk.*
>
> —Anonymous

Every wise elder will opine that "things will happen, and people will say stuff." The trauma of previous events will profoundly distort our view of possible possibilities. Memories of our past lead to natural yet irrational frustration, depression, anger, and self-deprecation. Stuff happens. Understand that we are wrestling with painful memories, traumatic circumstances, biased influences, and misleading triggers. Confronting our traumas and awareness of these factors is always the first step. Second, there will always be negative voices even from loved ones. They have all seen this movie once too often. Those voices are just there to distract you and cause you to stop the race. During the final yards of his marathon, some onlookers smirked and belittled Akhwari's efforts after twenty-six miles of perseverance. John would later chuckle that people discouraging his last trek to the finish line *were not even running in the race.*

Keep running

> *Even youths grow tired and weary, and young men stumble and fall; but those who hope in the* LORD *will renew their strength. They will soar on wings like eagles; they will run and not grow weary. They will walk and not be faint.*
>
> —Isaiah 40:30–31

Marathoner John Akhwari endured numerous stumbles and debilitating injuries running in the oxygen-depleted air of Mexico City. Yet even as many around him dropped out, he kept running. With no chance of attaining a medal, just finishing the race was victory enough. He continued as long as he could put one foot in front of the other. He just kept running. His experience has become a metaphor for perseverance and resilience. Woody Allen once said that 80 percent of achievement comes from just showing up and keeping running. We see the finish line far in the distance, 26.2 miles ahead, not realizing that all we can do is take one step and then another. The Bible keeps exhorting us to take action and then another. Just keep running.

- When no one invests in you, invest in yourself. *Keep running.*
- When no one believes in you, believe in yourself. *Keep running.*
- When no results are visible, *keep showing up* until you *see* results. *Keep running.*
- If no results appear for a long time, remember there will be no results unless you keep running.
- *80 percent of achievement is to keep running!*

We must not let impatience ruin the possibility. When we don't feel like it, take a step and then another. Every step brings us closer as this race is a marathon, not a sprint. The goal may be a place we cannot see, but this is the definition of *faith* as evidence of things unseen.

A journey of 1,000 miles begins with a single step. (Lao Tzu)

Grit means the revelation that failure is not a permanent condition. Perseverance implies the willingness to fail, open to the likelihood of getting it wrong but still stubborn enough to not give up. People who quit will often say that they have tried everything. They have tried everything—everything but keep running, everything but courage, everything but heart, everything but faith. Even if you fail, so what! Failure is quitting. Failure does not disqualify you, quitting does. Commitment will get you started. Grit will get you finished. Greatness is the culmination of many doable mundane, boring little acts. *You will enter a race metaphorically on your journey to achieve your goals.* Unfortunately, there will come a time when you feel that you have lost this race, but resilience means rejecting this reality because the race is not over. You must embrace the paradox that you can win the race even if you don't cross the finish line first. You will be a winner simply by finishing the race. *Just keep running until you finish the damned race!*

7

___

Changing Your Habits / Making Healthy Choices

Motivation gets you started. Habits keep you going.
—Jim Rohn

Getting released from cycles of compulsion (i.e., changing our habits) in this context ultimately involves change—and change terrifies us. Change requires letting go of what you know and embracing the unknown! Changing a pattern consists in assuming what you fear. It takes courage to let God transform you! It takes even more courage to start and stick with the process of changing yourself. We've just demonstrated that our present surrounding community probably will not support or encourage us. Often they are part of the problem! Change in any context involves not only what we gain but what we lose. We hold on to what we are used to, what is comfortable because it's all we know. Often we think what we don't know, the unknown, is from the devil! Thus, we refuse to allow God to change us. We may faithfully recite, "Old things pass away, and all things become new," but the truth is we don't want to lose control. We would rather die than lose control.

Yet at some point, our bondage situation, that addiction, that toxic relationship, that destructive habit gets so traumatic that we cry out for relief. We cry out for change. We cry out for change—only to discover that we are terrified of what God might change us into! So the smartest of us will intellectualize, preaching change to ourselves from the intellect, hoping it travels to the heart. But Jesus says, "*Just do what I have been saying. Just look at yourself, change your heart and let it travel to your intellect.*"

The state of our lives, good or bad, is wholly a result of our decisions. Our choices control our effective recovery and growth. Even when we are given clear strategies and processes to achieve, thrive, and recover from mistakes, we often fall short. Thus, effective change, recovery, and growth to mature fulfillment establish positive routines or habits of good behaviors—that is, replace bad habits with good ones. Jesus demonstrated identifiable patterns and habits. Likewise, every successfully recovered addict, every successful person will tell us that their key to growth is the habits they follow regularly, but this process is more straightforward said than done.

What is a habit?

The dictionary defines a *habit* as a routine of behavior, repeated regularly, that tends to occur subconsciously. Habits are ingrained activities that have become natural impulse actions done without thinking because of continued repetition. The movements cause a release in our brains of neurohormones, such as adrenaline, making these actions far more *effective* than usual. "Effective" action means these activities elevate the quality of our lives, helping us grow toward our goals that produce fruit in our spiritual and practical lives.

Habits affect our decisions

Old habits are hard to break, while new practices are hard to establish because our behavioral patterns are controlled by our human emotional urges, passions, and impulses. These neurological impulses can work against us by strongly influencing our decisions. Realize that decisions are never made in a moment in time. Decisions—good or bad, constructive or destructive—are rooted in our character. Thus, everything we desire—our growth, our control over negative urges, our elevation of positive instincts, our ability to establish good habits, our ability to maintain recovery and forward progress—is dependent on our character and our practices. That is, good character and good habits always result in good outcomes.

What is character?

Character is not inherited or some gift from above. It is not talent or ability. Character is built, and it is made with hard work, and nature and habits will form and drive our behavior. We show up every time through the routine practices with integrity to do what we promise. The most talented players are never the ultimate winners. The winners are those who practice and perform the routine over and over.

Habits are not willpower

Although it may seem logical, good habits are not the result of "willpower," self-control, or trying hard. (Good habits result from grit—a determination to do small simple things.) The Bible tells us to surrender, believe in a power greater than ourselves, and allow the Holy Spirit to help us and empower us. Willpower means doing things out of our own will for many of us. The Bible teaches simple things, little things repeatedly—repeatedly. We repeat the exclaim "*a day at a time.*" Thus, that is the process of establishing good habits.

Making healthy choices

> *We are born looking like our parents. We will die*
> *looking like our choices and decisions.*
> —Ademola Abidoye

> *But if serving the* Lord *seems undesirable to you, then*
> choose for yourselves *this day whom you will serve, whether*
> *the gods your ancestors served beyond the Euphrates or the*

gods of the Amorites, in whose land you are living. But as
for me and my household, we will serve the LORD.
—Joshua 24:15

When caught in a storm of unfortunate circumstances, we feel victimized or cursed. In moments of stress and crises, we make foolish choices, making decisions, choosing lifestyles and actions that are self-destructive. Beyond the fact that we have often made bad choices for ourselves, those choices also affect others. Even as victims, we need to understand that someone else made choices that affected or exploited us. Thus, our natural victim mentality and feelings of powerlessness are distortions that belie the fact that we always have a choice. The revelation and understanding of this, its acceptance and embrace, can greatly empower us. We need to be seeking an account of the options available. This understanding can transform us from persons who are reactive to proactive persons. In the end, we always serve the choices we have made.

Life is 10% what happened and 90% how
we react. (Chuck Swindoll)

Our ability to think always leads to the ability to choose, but our choices and decisions are not rationally determined among available options but are primarily influenced and controlled by the emotions and traumas we have experienced. If you think back to a baby, you realize that the child has a full menu of emotions long before that baby can reason. Essentially, the emotional part of the brain is formed before the thinking part of the brain—that is, we learn to feel before we know to think. Our emotions can easily override thinking, reason, and logic. As the child grows, they can feel sadness, joy, *anger,* pain, resentment, and jealousy. The child must learn and be taught to understand and control those emotions. Every piece of information and every experience we endure has a feeling attached.

As we go forth making the critical decisions of our lives, it is incredible how our feelings/emotions and our flesh affect our choices. We hurt or are in pain. We are defensive, protective, or jealous/

resentful/angry. We are deeply attracted to someone, lust for power, sex, money, and position. Usually very legitimate feelings/emotions color and influence our decisions, but quite often, we have strong desires and compulsions inside us that affect our decision-making process. In short, we simply want what we want, and these compulsions/desires go up and down in their intensity; and as these influences shift and change, our decisions will also change. Thus, though we are well-versed in biblical wisdom and know better, we still can make some "dumb," often regrettable decisions.

Often after multiple traumatic events, like losing a loved one, we will desensitize, becoming emotionless. This is what we call burying the emotion alive. Once again, when you suppress your feeling, your issue, your vulnerability, in due time, under the right conditions and circumstances, it will always resurrect. It resurrects at the worst possible moment to wreak havoc in your life and the lives of your loved ones. Often the emotion or the issue will renew in some disguise of the original manifestation but with the exact root causes. Finally, we often mask our vulnerabilities and traumas, convincing ourselves that we have conquered our demons and giving them even more power.

> We need to educate our emotions because they were meant to bless us. But left uneducated, our feelings begin to direct our thinking, guide our feelings, determine our direction and thus control our lives. (Dr. A. R. Bernard)

Capturing our thoughts

> *As a man thinks in his heart, so is he.*
>
> —Proverbs 23:7

In Corinthians 10:15, the Bible demands that we "*bring into captivity every thought to the obedience of Christ.*" But this is such a daunting task—easier said than done! Psychologists estimate we think sixty thousand thoughts in a single day, with over 98 percent of them being the same as yesterday. They are wholly unproductive—useless fantasy, wandering, meandering, and uncontrolled notions. The overwhelming majority are negative. Negative thoughts push you mentally backward toward defeat, treachery, and selfish, covetous, lustful compulsion by our very nature. By repeating messages two dozen times, advertising execs can influence your subconscious mind into making a "buy" decision. Imagine the negative impact on your actions, peace of mind, and ability to accomplish by manipulating and influencing the twenty-two million thoughts that flash through your mind in a single year? The thought is staggering.

On the other hand, think of the righteous impact, the positive effects, the prosperity and effective growth that could be sustained on your life, your marriage, your family, your business, your ministry, etc., by recalibrating, directing, and focusing just a portion of your "thought volume"? Yet the paradoxical belief in the gospel of Jesus Christ concludes that the only reason people don't have victory in their lives is that they have not decided to be victorious. (A paradox is a statement that does not seem logical yet accurate.) God gives you that power to determine and purpose, the power ability to be saved, delivered, redeemed, and blessed. Thus, that power to decide is made even more potent with information. The decision is made more potent beyond our initial understanding by knowledge.

8

Self-Denial

*Then Jesus said to His disciples, "If anyone desires to come after
Me, let him deny himself, take up his cross, and follow Me."*
—Mark 8:34; Matthew 16:24; Luke 9:23

Christians are quick to testify about victory over our demons, yet no one ever celebrates denial of ourselves. Truthfully, self-denial is antithetical to everything we desire; and yet Jesus repeatedly begs, demands, implores us to do just that! Following Christ will *always* involve a mental process of self-denial and sacrifice. Self-denial is the decision to deny ourselves something we would like, something we crave and believe we cannot live without. Self-denial or self-sacrifice is an act of letting go of the self as with altruistic abstinence—the willingness to forgo personal pleasures or undergo personal trials to pursue the increased good of another.

God's readiness to give and forgive is now public. Salvation's available for everyone! We're being shown how to turn our backs on a godless, indulgent life and how to take on a God-filled, God-honoring life. This new life is starting right now and is whetting our appetites for the glorious day when our great God and Savior, Jesus Christ, appears. He offered himself as a sacrifice to free us from a dark, rebellious life into this good, pure life, making us a people he can be proud of, energetic in goodness. (Titus 2: 11–14 MSG)

A longing for Egypt

That night all the members of the community raised their voices and wept aloud. All the Israelites grumbled against Moses and Aaron, and the whole assembly said to them, "If only we had died in Egypt! Or in this wilderness! Why is the LORD bringing us to this land only to let us fall by the sword? Our wives and children will be taken as plunder. Wouldn't it be better for us to go back to Egypt?" And they said to each other, "We should choose a leader and go back to Egypt."
—Numbers 14:1–4

We struggle with self-denial because we tend to focus on ending the old and not beginning the new. We spend all our energy mourning what we lost, not what we gained. Our new beginning always starts with a longing for the old. Thus, we can't get to the Promised Land while still obsessing about Egypt!

But God wants us to self-deny the habits of old, the destructive cycles that have medicated us in our misery, making us coconspirators to our bondage! We have become our most effective enablers, but without a vision of our future, we are destined to return to our past. All we know is the Egypt we are leaving. Moses provided the Hebrew enslaved people with a prophetic vision of the place they were going—a promised land.

Prayer

O God, give us the strength to focus on moving forward, forgetting the former things and pressing onward to the high calling you have set before us. Give us eyes to see and ears to hear your voice in the wilderness, calling us forward to the place we are destined to be—a promised land. Amen.

Practicing self-denial

Practicing self-denial may often seem like an impossibility. Have you ever practiced the discipline of fasting? Though many agree with the advantages of prayer, there remains debate about fasting as a discipline. Yet Jesus tells us to fast and pray repeatedly. Fasting is a practice of refraining from everyday activities to focus our attention on Christ. Most commonly, fasting is avoiding food for specific periods, but we can fast other things.

> So, He said to them, "This kind can come out by nothing but prayer and fasting." (Mark 9:29)

We may intellectually understand and agree with the call for self-denial. We even see the benefit in obeying Christ even if it contradicts our deep desires. We pray for the strength to obey and dispute our longings, but compulsion is an addictive mental force that causes us to falter. It is tough to say no when we have every means to satisfy ourselves. There are no "virtue points" for saying no to ourselves. Fasting is a discipline that helps us *practice* saying no to ourselves. It helps us learn the habit of setting aside our desires to make room for pursuing God's will.

Prayer

> I confess, Lord, that I often avoid doing the good that I would like to do. I admit that I regularly violate your commands—despite my best intentions. Transform me, making me new, so I can do what is good and right for myself and obey your will. Amen.

Self-denial as self-care

Most of us never consider self-care until crisis or trauma forces us—addiction, depression, etc.—robbing us of peace of mind and body. *God can use problems to confront us in revelations we have never considered.* Self-care is any activity we do deliberately to enhance our mental, emotional, and physical health. We can find greater freedom and joy in these self-care activities in him. Self-denial is a vital part of the process of self-care. No self-denial, no self-care.

We hesitate to self-deny because of an unspoken fear that we can't live without the destructive things that satisfy us. Self-denial as self-care puts us back in charge of our thoughts and feelings rather than being at the mercy of thoughts and feelings! We have wasted so much time obsessing about something that never satisfied us, which kills us long-term. Self-denial returns power over things that had dominion over us. We live in fear of being without what medicates us from pain, never considering that self-denial will eventually heal us from pain.

> Jesus said, "Are you tired? Worn out and burned out on religion? Come to me. Get away with me, and you'll recover your life. I'll show you how to take a real rest. Walk with me and work with me—watch how I do it. Learn the unforced rhythms of grace. I won't lay anything heavy or ill-fitting on you. Keep company with me, and you'll learn to live freely and lightly." (Matthew 11:26–30 MSG)

Prayer

> O God, we depend upon you, humbling ourselves before you, recognizing all that you have done for us and will do for us. Give us strength, O God, to deny those things that would cause us harm and embrace those things that bring us life. Reveal the blessings that you have in store if we obey your word. Amen.

9

Boundaries for Growth

The boundary lines have fallen for me in pleasant places; indeed, I have a delightful inheritance.

—Psalm 16:6

Jackson Bermudez, a muscular bear of a man, darkly handsome and smooth-talking, had a reputation as a "ladies man" in his lower eastside NYC neighborhood. Converted to Christianity, discipleship for Jackson was a constant struggle of confronting inappropriate urges and digesting criticism for many of his prior beliefs and values. The restrictions on masturbation and innocent philandering with multiple women seemed to lessen his masculinity and subdue his feelings of freedom. Jackson's self-identity and pride were tied to his urge to manifest this distorted view of manhood. Although he enthusiastically presented himself as an avid Christian believer, he mentally hesitated to set boundaries, resist flirtatious comments, and repent of an improper thought life. Biblical instruction and wisdom, beneficial in the long run, are often paradoxical to our popular culture. We get stuck and caught in compulsive cycles because we intentionally refuse to set limitations on certain behaviors until it's too late. Boundaries are often viewed instinctively as negatives—barriers, prison bars, roadblocks—all the things we can't do. Talking with men about boundaries and limitations, particularly sexual, is often met with eye rolls and smirks. I was one of those men.

I once was convinced my freedoms would likewise be suppressed by restricting the small things that lead to big compulsions, yet with maturity, I understood these restraints were the process of developing strength, endurance, and abilities. Every athlete realizes that regular daily workouts (i.e., purposeful resistance and pressure) build muscle mass. Likewise, the wise boundaries we regularly observe, set by God, are directly intended for our *growth*—not to keep us from having a good time or getting blessed! They are the path to blessing. Frankly, we will not accomplish our dreams and visions without establishing boundaries for growth.

What are boundaries?

A boundary is a line/marker, border, or frontier designating division, or the limit of one thing from another, determining who and what is an entity. For our purposes, boundaries are

- the actions we won't do,
- the places we won't go, and
- the thoughts we try to cast out of our minds.

Personal boundaries are guidelines, rules, and limits created by a person to identify for themselves what is reasonable, safe, and permissible. Boundaries determine what behaviors of others we will tolerate and our response when someone steps outside those limits. The physical boundaries are much easier to maintain than the mental boundaries. Unfortunately, our minds are programmed to drift onto topics and into stimulating but harmful and inappropriate areas. Consequently, we need to focus on awareness and understanding that these topics of thought lead to eventual adverse outcomes. Please realize that the most powerful and controlling habits make us feel good and assuage our feelings of inadequacy. We get personal with those habits, taking ownership, protecting, and covering those habits. Once we realize modern culture tacitly applauds certain behaviors, we no longer think of them as wrong. We think, *"I mean they don't hurt anyone."*

As long as our compulsive behavior, our sin, is our friend, we will not stop. As long as we deny that little things control our lives, we will not stop. When we fail to see the long-term destructive consequences of our sin, we only see its immediate gratification, its short-term burst of pleasure, and it is hard to kill what we love. Further, admission of the problem and confession is acceptable, but that won't fix the problem. That can only be accomplished when we set simple small boundaries set in stone. The bigger more difficult ones can evolve later.

Divine boundaries

> *The Lord God took the man and put him in the Garden of Eden to work it and take care of it. And the Lord God commanded the man, "You are free to eat from any tree in the garden; but you must not eat from the tree of the knowledge of good and evil, for when you eat from it, you will certainly die."*
> —Genesis 2:15–17

Divine boundaries are prophetic (i.e., preventing us from unapparent long-term disaster down the road). God told Adam and Eve not to eat from the fruit from the tree of the knowledge of good and evil. *After the fall*, we realize nothing good came from this disobedience. Second, divine boundaries are process-oriented. Eventually, the knowledge of good and evil would benefit Adam and Eve with maturity, experience, and understanding of that level of revelation. For example, restricting my eight-year-old grandson from driving the car doesn't mean he will never learn to drive. It means he's not ready, mature enough, at eight years old. Back in the garden, Adam and Eve complained of boundaries intended to *"keep (them) from being like God, knowing good and evil"* (Genesis 3:5). Today nothing has changed as we think God wants to take away our fun. Thus, we sprint down a path leading to destructive, inappropriate, and even deadly compulsions. The excuses we make are astounding as our justification for this tortuous path. Listen to a few examples I have heard:

- "No problem. I can handle it."
- "This is who I am."
- "I need to celebrate my victory!"
- "I need to medicate my pain."
- "I need to cover over this wounded heart."
- "I am just admiring her beauty. That can't be wrong!"
- "God has called me to save him/her."

Embrace the boundary

In our "me-oriented" society, giving into carnal desires is encouraged and considered a sign of strength and freedom. Yet the Bible warns that many things are permissible, available, doable, and possible, but not many things are beneficial or expedient (1 Corinthians 10:23). Despite the carnal logic of our world, purity remains an intentional choice. Ultimately, sobriety is a choice. Thus, embracing boundaries is also a choice—difficult though it may be at first. The weightlifter only focuses on the muscles that will bulge, not the donuts he is missing! We must stop focusing on what we can't do. We must become growth-focused.

Though our popular manhood culture believes slavery to our desires is a form of potent power, it's nothing but slavery, pure and simple. Once I became acutely aware of my behavior in certain situations, I began to revile the carnal urges that seemed beyond my control, outside my ability to say no. It was as if some outside force had captured my willpower. I adjusted my belief system to redetermining my boundaries—what's okay and not okay. Reexamining my belief systems, I tried to determine the proper limits. Aristotle once said, *"Even virtue becomes vice when taken to the extreme."* The critical need for a balanced outlook implies the establishment of clear boundaries. Even good things and blessings, when embraced without limitation, will become a curse. Confidence without borders becomes pride. Self-esteem without limits becomes conceit. Love of race quickly becomes racism without boundary.

What's okay and what's not okay!

Setting boundaries is ultimately a value judgment. The most important key to understanding the concept is not letting our urges and compulsions determine our boundaries. The boundaries essentially shape our lives; we set the "yes" and the "no" in stone. Without boundaries, we have no definition, no character and integrity. I would often confront men by demanding, "*What do you stand for? If you don't know, then you will stand for anything!*" Some can drink alcohol responsibly, yet once that ability to drink becomes an urge, the vulnerability to compulsive drinking is real. We must realize that our urges, the compulsions that captivate us, are obvious boundaries, markers that we must not pass. Once these limitations are given and we become compulsive, our identity becomes the condition that controls us. At that point, our growth and human development are turned away from areas we otherwise would be striving for.

Growth-focused boundaries

Firstly, *growth* is defined as developing, maturing, and increasing spiritual, mental, emotional, and physical stature and size. As discussed throughout this book, development involves intentionally pursuing *repeated* cycles of specific actions and denying certain other activities. God sets boundless goals and dreams as the endpoint. In sync with God's purpose for us in our lives, we embrace these dreams and goals for ourselves. In his Word, God gives practical strategy as action steps to achieve these dreams. The action steps are what we refer to as "process." Again, the process involves the boundaries of both things you do and the things you do not do—that is, to achieve boundless dreams, we must embrace certain limitations.

Once again, we must mature to view boundaries as blessings that cause us to grow. We develop muscles through boundaries. We grow tall buildings by setting limits. God wants us to grow up and not sideways. The boundary is not a limitation but an opportunity. Once again, we control urges and irresponsible desires by first focusing on the goal and then, second, on the boundaries. A person can only be filled full or *fulfilled* if there is a boundary or top to our "gas" tank. Removing the top means it will never be crammed full. Thus, persons with no limitations always feel unfulfilled and empty. Determination to achieve a goal also involves clear actions—even good actions—we will not do.

Four steps to setting boundaries

Dr. Henry Cloud and Dr. John Townsend have prepared excellent steps for setting boundaries in their book *Boundaries: When to Say Yes. How to Say No to Take Control of Your Life.*[20]

1. "Attend" or decide.

> Our brains must *attend* to the relevant stuff. When we set goals, we focus all our attention on that goal. Thus, this step involves decision, management, organizing, and taking charge of developing and reaching this goal. This leads to the power of prayer. Praying is actually "stop and focus" on a topic. Direct your *attention* to a topic.

> Hear my cry, O God; *attend unto my prayer.* From the end of the earth will I cry unto thee, when my heart is overwhelmed: lead me to the rock that is higher than I. Thou hast been a shelter for me and a strong tower from the enemy. (Psalm 61 KJV)

> There is a phrase—"to pay attention." The process of attention is an investment of time and energy and focus. Our brains cannot deal with clutter. We must ask ourselves, *"What are the four things that need to be attended to or focused on?"*

---

[20] Henry Cloud & John Townsend, *Boundaries: When to Say Yes. How to Say No to Take Control of Your Life* (Zondervan, 1992).

2. Focus on the one.

   Cloud and Townsend declare that multitasking is a fallacy as far as brain science goes. Achievement relies on a strict hierarchy of focus. We must guard against being unfocused and schizophrenic minds to overcome compulsive desires. The brain must attend to one activity and shut everything out for the best result. When performing one action, the brain is firing on all cylinders—in the flow, creativity, practical, problem solving, and adapting modes. When you pause one activity and shift to start another action, even for only two minutes, when you return to the first activity, you do not start back up at the same pace you left off. Even though you have left the first activity for only two minutes, the net effect is a twenty-minute delay due to the time it takes to ramp up to the same flow speed as when you paused. To get anywhere, we have to be able to shut other things out and focus—on a marriage, on a vision, a problem.

3. Keep it current.

   Keep your goal for achievement in front of you. This means "building the now." Allegorically, this means determining goals, we must "plant and nourish" our actions in a repeating manner—that is, we are developing habits. The growth of a plant does not occur by dipping it into the wet dirt once a week. We must plant and nourish our actions and clear, consistent, repeated routines so these routines can take roots.

4. Embrace limits.

   Embracing limits means starving your appetite. This sounds severe, but you get hungrier when you satisfy your hunger. Our appetite for sin means that when we feed it, the need grows. We must stop this sense of nibbling around the edges or getting close to a line we say we won't cross. This attitude ignores or devalues the power of temptation. Our passion must be removing the temptation. This removal of an attractive lure is the key to self-discipline.

Conclusion

Once again, trying to do many things well and setting many boundaries is not recommended. Rather than doing a few things very well, we try to do everything simultaneously. The problem is that we are human and limited. *Better to be known for a few things we do well than the many things we do mediocre.* God is God. You are not. Rely on mentors. God sent someone else to support you in the area of their gifting. He sent a wife, and he sent helpers, but we are so selfish that we cannot accept the help. *Stay in your lane.* Trusting God with our limits and boundaries has been with us since the garden of Eden. This is an applied theology of limits.

10

Seven Steps to Becoming Unstuck

1. *Decide.* Decide if you *want* to change. Often you're *forced* to change, but be careful your condition hasn't become normative. You may have become comfortable in your mess, and change is terrifying. Your actions to change must be intentional. Nothing changes if there are no changes, so don't sit waiting for something to happen. Try to focus on positive things you enjoy and give you purpose. Realize that your reaction to situations begins with the thoughts and ideas you create. You always have the choice to create new ones. Rather than dwelling on what can go wrong, focus on new possibilities.

2. *Take a step*—even if it's a small step. Small steps become significant steps. Focus on the step. Psalm 37:23: "*The Lord directs the steps of good men. He delights in each step they take.*" We think in giant leaps, but God says to take a step, *not a leap.* If you live in a community that supports your dysfunction, make an effort to change the people who pour into you. Rather than arguing with your neighbors about moving forward, surround yourself with those who will move forward with you. Try leaving people who drain you, and be around people who pour into you.

3. *Move forward.* Go in a *forward* direction. We get frustrated by no movement, so do something. *Do something.* Meet new people. *Listen.* Wear new clothes. Change something. Second letter to the Corinthians 5:17: "*Therefore if any man is in Christ, he is a new creature: old things are passed away; behold, all things become new.*" Search for opportunities to figure out what to do with your life. You are a valuable human being with fundamental skills. Try committing to *yourself.* You should constantly be scanning the horizon to see how you can best offer those skills.

4. *Embrace new.* Embrace change. Take positive risks. Understand that new beginnings may feel like endings because old is comfortable. New is frightening/terrifying, but change requires letting go and embracing the unknown. We hold onto what we are used to, what is satisfied, what we know. The difference is, by definition, what we don't know—embracing the unknown because change takes courage.

5. *Clear the negative.* Negativity makes you feel stuck. Get away from toxic people—who gossip, criticize, waste your time, are jealous, are victimized, don't care, and are self-centered. They will always disappoint you. Make sure you're taking care of yourself. If you're tired and dehydrated, it's only natural to think negative thoughts and begin to feel so lost in life. The body and the mind are related, and your brain will pull from your physical state to think ideas about your physical feelings.

6. *Do not overthink.* (Stop stressing about what can go wrong.) You do not control everything. Let go and let *God.* Just do it. We do all kinds of dangerous, risky things with stupid faith. Yet when God tells you to do positive things, we rationalize what can "go wrong"! Do what God tells you to do. Take a God risk.

7. *Have vision*—what you see happening in your mind will occur in your life. Dr. Bernard always said, "Without a vision of your future, you are destined to return to your

past." *But* your future happens at the right time, in the right place, for the right reasons. If one way does not work, *maybe it was not meant for you.* Try something else. Change occurs in a different order at an additional time than you imagine.

11

The Ten Steps to Emotional Health

The unexamined life is not worth living.

—Socrates

An emotionally unhealthy person always deals with feelings of being stuck in unproductive, often destructive ways, yet everyone is vulnerable to being emotionally immature. Humans commonly display only 15 percent of our emotional makeup above the surface like an iceberg. Fully 85 percent of our character, integrity, and emotional makeup remain hidden below the surface, out of view and consideration. Sadly, most of our focus and attention, Christian or secular, is directed to that 15 percent visible even though our character and well-being flow from the 85 percent hidden, untouched by God, and unexamined by our conscience.

I believe a mature embrace of the Christian faith produces profound, positive change, yet despite surface appearances, so often it does not. The ten steps to emotional health attempt to dig beneath the "good Christian" veneer to examine the layers of our lives God has not yet touched—layers we have concealed and avoided. These layers of our emotions have left us emotionally and spiritually immature. Hopefully, this effort will unearth and discuss those layers and present a practical model of self-examination and the steps to transformation (see below) into emotional and spiritual health, producing a faith charged with authenticity, contemplation, and a hunger for God.

Ten Steps to Emotional Health

1. Recognize, understand, and manage our feelings and emotions.
2. Proactive compassion for others (not reactive emotion).
3. Accountable and in the community (isolation is an enemy strategy).
4. Break free from self-destructive patterns.
5. Understand our past and how it impacts our present.
6. Express our thoughts and feelings to others clearly and respectfully.
7. Love others without changing them.
8. Resolve conflicts intentionally.
9. Sober self-assessment.
10. Deal with loss maturely, mourning/grieving well.

1. Sober self-assessment

> *Who am I, O Sovereign LORD, and what is my*
> *family that you have brought me this far?*
> —2 Samuel 7:18

The first command of Jesus, the minister, was "to repent" (*metanoeo*)—not a mere confession but a sober self-examination and inward reconsideration of our true nature. Yet this moral self-judgment challenges our instinct to seek affirmation/approval, know and be known, and be liked. We fear our deepest secrets and shortcomings, thus presenting a veiled image, masking our true selves. Therefore, we naturally disguise our hurts, addictions and compulsions, embarrassing faults and weaknesses, and our vulnerabilities. And while our "stuff" remains buried behind this mask, the issues fester, often multiplying like a fungus unchecked.

Worse, dysfunctional people, masking their issues, attract other dysfunctional people who are too blind to see beyond their masks. Relationships progress between strangers who *never* reveal themselves to each other. *Thus, couples may see each other physically naked while never being transparent or showing their actual characters.* Without transparent relationships, it's no surprise that the rates of divorce and unhappy marriages are so high for Christians and secular folk alike.

When you bury your issues alive, burying them without honestly killing them, in due time, they will resurrect again at the worst possible moment to wreak havoc in your life and the lives of your loved ones. That buried stuff renews in differing manifestations of the original issue but with the exact root causes. Sadly, as long as the mask remains in place, we convince ourselves that we have conquered our demons. Thus, Jesus, the healer, cannot heal our wounds.

Worse still, the church still suffers from instances of hypocrisy. We can destroy other people inside and outside the church while secretly struggling with similar issues. Often, like homosexuals in the military, we "don't ask, don't tell." The church sets a standard of holiness that is admirable and scriptural, yet when we compare ourselves to expectations, we fall short. Realizing our ugly nakedness, we are ashamed and hide (*remember Adam's reply to God*). We move forward like nothing ever happened, knowing deep within our consciousness that we are less than what we outwardly appear. Thus, sitting in church, we live in caves of secrecy, with all of us having something in us that we don't want to be exposed to. But there can be no healing in hiding. To heal, you have to tell. You cannot be fully loved unless you are fully known.

2. Understand our past and how it impacts our present

> *Yet He does not leave the guilty unpunished; He punishes the children and their children for the sin of the fathers to the third and fourth generation.*
>
> —Exodus 34:7

Every young boy, every child, grows up and takes cues on behaving from those around him. Every child searches for and longs for attention and acts in a manner that reflects the image of the adults that care for them. Adam was made in the image and likeness of his father, yet Adam falls into sin; and thus, the sons and daughters of Adam become a selfish, sinful reflection of the image of their father. *Without them even knowing it, they have been imprinted by the nature of their forefathers, often wounded by his arrows or emboldened by his passions and lustful endeavors. Thus, a cycle of sin and pain is perpetuated.*

3. Recognize, understand, and manage our feelings and emotions.

> *O, what a wretched man I am! Who will*
> *rescue me from this body of death?*
> —Romans 7:24

A baby emerges from the womb with the ability to feel emotion long before it learns to understand the sentiment. Feelings of joy, fear, irritation, etc., are experienced by the child before rational thought or cognitive recognition. Thus, it is natural for our emotions and how we feel to easily override our thinking, reason, and logic. Second, sincere commitment to Christ exempts us from remaining deeply unhealthy emotional beings, subject to full, irrational swings in temperament and well-being. Finally, rarely are the steps taken toward establishing models of vibrant health.

For example, Jesus is rarely presented as a model of emotional health despite being fully human. Often the image is of a stoic, distant Jesus, sinless and perfect. Scriptures give a far more comprehensive range of emotional personality traits beyond love/passion. Jesus shows joy/laughter, grief/sorrow, the realization of loss, anger, irritation, resentment, depression, stress, anxiety, and conflict. As a man in numerous personal, commercial, and political relationships, he was perceived as familiar and friendly, compassionate and caring, inspirational and motivational, innocent yet flirtatious, rebellious, confrontational and almost insulting, slick and political, revolutionary, entrepreneurial, practical, even dreamy. He confused, mystified, disillusioned, disappointed, angered, and even terrified many including his own family, followers, and disciples, living his calling under enormous emotional and psychological pressure. How did he cope and survive, let alone overcome? Can Jesus be our model?

Though quiet and purposeful in enduring abuse, Jesus experienced the typical human reactions indicative of his situation. Gethsemane shows a man on a mission, feeling conflicted, torn, fearful, divided, hesitant, and experiencing extreme emotional stress and anxiety. Examine the moving process, the prayers, and the attitude he used to recognize his strategies for dealing, confronting, and overcoming his emotions.

God's first command was "Let there be light." The prophetic description of Jesus was as a Great Light and the Wonderful Counselor. Firstly, in every strategic action plan, illuminate/recognize the truths/information affecting your emotional state. Take off the mask, and acknowledge the emotions. *Every piece of information received, true or false, has a feeling attached.* You cannot manage that which you do not own.

4. Break free from self-destructive patterns.

> *Forgetting what is behind and straining toward what is*
> *ahead, I press on toward the goal of winning the prize for*
> *which God has called me heavenward in Christ Jesus.*
> —Philippians 3:13–14

The cycle is God's strategy and platform for the growth and development of life. God ordained our existence on spinning planets in revolving galaxies in cycling universes. The circadian rhythm of a twenty-four-hour day evolves into months, years, and repeating seasons, allowing all living things to grow and develop. Our lives, generations, and legacies are composed of these rhythmic cycles.

> As long as the earth endures, seedtime and
> harvest, cold and heat, summer, and winter, day
> and night will never cease. (Genesis 8:22)

Yet the enemy imitates this effective process in corrupting us with evil, destructive cycles and patterns. Worse, our struggles are compounded and passed through generations. Thus, sin and the issues of life, even diseases and afflictions, often come in cycles, passed down through generations.

Breaking the cycle

1. Realize you are on a journey in a season.
2. Plant a seed (no seed no harvest).
3. You build either stumbling blocks or stepping-stones.
4. Sow to the Spirit. Reap what you plant or sow.
5. Patience, trust, and fret not. (Trouble will come.)
6. Make moral choices, quality choices. The quality of my choices determines the quality of my harvest.
    *   Maturity is delaying gratification.
    *   Immaturity—not delaying, ignorance of the consequences.
7. The quantity of my nos determines the quality of my yeses.
8. Joy in the journey—yesterday is history, tomorrow in the hands of God.
9. Understand the process of healing.

5. Being in the community and accountable. (Isolation is an enemy strategy.)

> *Let us not give up meeting together, as some are in the*
> *habit of doing, but let us encourage one another—and*
> *all the more as you see the Day approaching.*
> —Hebrews 10:25 (NIV)

Although routine quiet, personal time alone is healthy, God has a spiritual and practical purpose for his desire that man is in a *positive* relationship and a positive community. Unfortunately, our thinking, amid isolation, is naturally flawed and selfish. While it is crucial to spend time alone with God in monologue and, hopefully, dialogue, it is deadly and destructive to isolate and address issues, problems, and destiny exclusive of relationships. That is why the family and the church are so vital to the well-being of man in our society. That is why God says in the very beginning that it is not suitable for man to be alone. The most successful process strategy for generating good habits, emotional stability, and self-development is surrounded by a positive community accountable to a godly authority figure.

6. Express our thoughts and feelings to others clearly and respectfully.

> *"Come now, let us reason together," says the LORD. "Though your sins are like scarlet, they shall be as white as snow; though they are red as crimson, they shall be like wool."*
> —Isaiah 1:18

The biggest problem affecting relationships, even Christian relationships, is the ability, willingness, and essential need to communicate. Most couples echo the same frustration over the desire to communicate more effectively. Resolution and the stress attached cannot occur without effective communication. Please note that communication doesn't mean just blurting it all out either. Some things are hurtful and better left unsaid.

But we desperately need to develop some transparency with our mates about our thoughts and feelings if these relationships prosper. Through listening and sharing (i.e., communication), we create a satisfying bond of intimacy in our relationships.

7. Deal with loss maturely. Mourning/grieving well.

> *Jesus wept.*
> —John 11:35

Dealing with loss involves death and the emotional loss from divorce, job failure, disappointment, and disillusionment. Every time our confident expectations are destroyed, we experience a loss akin to a death of a loved one. Every time our comfort zone is ripped from us, we do not let go quickly, if at all. Factually most of us grieve and scream and moan and ache and pity ourselves. We want to die. Experiencing those feelings must not push us out of control into disastrous decision-making.

Emotionally healthy grieving/mourning of loss is part of the process of confronting/releasing the emotion so you can move on, yet unhealthy grieving allows stress, anxiety, or denial to dominate our well-being and decision-making in an often disastrous way. Mourning and grieving well is confronting, not covering unimaginable losses in a process allowing us to emerge on the other side.

8. Resolve conflicts intentionally.

> *Out of the same mouth come praise and cursing.*
> *My brothers, this should not be.*
> —James 3:10

There are as many ways to react to conflict in the house as personality types. Some people withdraw while others fight to the bitter end. They cannot stand to be wrong or lose, which drives their partner even farther away. Then again, others yield. They give up because it simply isn't worth the hassle. Peace in the house becomes a process of denial that any problem exists.

Yet according to the Word, a fourth reaction exists—each one giving up a little to try and meet in the middle. If you want a relationship to succeed, remember, the secret to the living is in the dying—the dying to self. Each person has died a little to "self in every successful relationship." Amid the dense city of our lives, you need to knock down some strongholds before a magnificent temple of relationship can be built in its place.

Here are six principles to follow in the process of working through the conflict:

- Adopt a learner's posture (i.e., learn from the experience of each conflict).
- Listen with your heart: "He whose ear listens to the 'life-giving reproof' will dwell among the wise" (Proverbs 15:31).
- Keep emotions under control: "The anger of man doesn't achieve the righteousness of God" (James 1:20).
- Think before you speak: No "mouths in motion" before your "mind is in gear."
- Focus on *your* part of the blame.
- Keep short accounts. Don't take days and days to address and resolve each conflict.

9. Proactive compassion for others (not reactive emotion)

> *Do not seek revenge or bear a grudge against one of your*
> *people, but love your neighbor as yourself. I am the LORD.*
> —Leviticus 19:18

Most folks confuse proactive compassion with reactive emotion. Proactive compassion is a decision that asks what is in the long-term best interest of a person. What is the best way of lovingly and gently conveying this? Further, is this the right time or situation to say anything other than attentive listening? Every person has emotions in reaction to an event. However, the expression of emotion can be a selfish display and upload of feelings with disastrous consequences.

10. Love others unconditionally.

> *When he saw the crowds, he had compassion on them because*
> *they were harassed and helpless, like sheep without a shepherd.*
> —Matthew 9:36

As Christians, instinctively we know that we must love others. Thus, we usually translate that love into wanting to change people for our concept of good. Emotionally, healthy loving involves compassion, incarnation, unconditional concern, bringing truth/light, and setting an example. Indeed, we desire that people change for the better, but we cannot impose change on anybody. Learn to be patient and live within limits. Jesus did not heal every person in Palestine. He did not raise every deserving dead person. He did not feed every hungry beggar or establish job development centers for the poor, yet he no doubt loved everyone. Christians sometimes feel that they have to take care of everybody except themselves. Jesus's command was to "follow me." *He took care of himself in preparation to lead.* He did not force anyone to follow and understood that not everyone would. He lived within limits but was compassionate and brought truth and light, setting an example that others could choose to follow.

> Self-care is not selfish. It is good steward-
> ship of the only gift I have—the gift of offering a
> healthy me to others. (Parker Palmer)

Subconsciously embedded in our evangelism and compassion is the unintentional implication that a person must change as a condition for our love and acceptance. We do not consciously intend to hang conditions on our passion, but our actions often convey that to the listener. However, it is only when a person knows that you love them unconditionally (i.e., without them changing) that they will consider changing. Change is only accurate for personal, sincere motivation and not to please someone else. Jesus, the Son of God, did not bribe people with promises of entry into heaven. Jesus empowered people to take healthy control of their emotional and spiritual lives.

About the Author

After many years as an architect and professional construction project manager, Martin A. Bowman has served as a licensed chaplain and counselor to those in crisis and men/women recovering from substance abuse for the last fifteen years. He has worked at NYC Rescue Mission, New York; Goodwill Rescue Mission, Newark, New Jersey; and Freedom House Inc., Clinton, New Jersey.

Since 2004, Martin and his wife, Rev. Angela Bowman, have operated Seasons of Purpose, consulting with New York, New Jersey, and New England area ministries and churches on the program, property development, and building issues.

Martin attends Primitive Christian Church on the Lower East Side (Pastor Marc Rivera). He and his wife lead the Worshipping Arts ministry, an urban community-oriented creative arts ministry, displaying the gospel through drama, music, dance, and spoken Word. He is a playwright, actor/choreographer, and devotional speaker on urban ministry themes.